WARNING

WARNING

THIS IS NOT A MOTIVATIONAL STORY

fousey

YOUSEF ERAKAT

WITH MARTIN SVENSSON AND LEIF ERIKSSON

PERMUTED
PRESS

A PERMUTED PRESS BOOK

ISBN: 978-1-68261-985-8
ISBN (eBook): 978-1-68261-986-5

Cover art by Cody Corcoran
Interior design and composition, Greg Johnson, Textbook Perfect

**PERMUTED
PRESS**

Permuted Press, LLC
New York • Nashville
permutedpress.com

Published in the United States of America
1 2 3 4 5 6 7 8 9 10

CONTENTS

"Cities don't change people.
People don't even change people.
We are who we are."

—HANK MOODY

*If you feel good and want to keep it that way,
you should probably stop reading now.*

You still have time to stop reading.

OK, suit yourself....

Don't say I didn't warn you.

TO WHOM IT MAY CONCERN...

I'm in hell. I'm living in a world where I wish I could disappear every day. I'm living in shame. I'm living in guilt. I wake up with no purpose, no idea what to do or how to do it.

Yesterday, when I talked to my mama on the phone, I said: "Everybody hates me." But like any other mother in the same situation, she tried to convince me that they don't.

Mama is very enthusiastic about life, so we often get into discussions. My baba actually got involved yesterday too. "The whole country hates Donald Trump, but you don't see him stopping." I guess he's right. It's just that since July 15, 2018, I haven't been the same. Partly because I feel so much regret about what I did, and partly because I'm always thinking about how, if I could just go back and do one thing different, I could change the course of my life forever.

The only thing that really animates me these days is when someone writes to say that they relate to me. I want people to know that I understand them. Not only for their sake, but for mine as well—because it makes me feel less alone. That's also the reason I'm writing this now. I hope we have something in common.

Yousef Erakat
Los Angeles, April 2020

"Beating heroin is child's play compared to beating your childhood."

—STEPHEN KING

FREMONT, CA 510

I become Nick's bitch.

My story begins at 32808 Bluebird Loop in Fremont, California, in the summer of 1997. What I remember most clearly about the two-story house is the living room where Baba used to sit up late at night, watching the news on the TV. I remember the kitchen, too, where Mama would be cooking up one Arabic dish or another (and usually sending an amazing aroma out onto the street) in her apron.

The bedroom I shared with my two older brothers, Mohammed and Ahmed, was on the second floor. My big sister, Noura, had the room beside ours, and our parents the one across from that. My parents were immigrants from Palestine and had arrived in the States without (even) a high school education, but Baba still managed to get a bank loan and start a deli in downtown San Francisco.

This was before Starbucks took over the world, so a whole bunch of people used to go to his deli for coffee or sandwiches. Despite that, he still had to work pretty much 24/7 just to stay afloat.

I went to work with him sometimes and had to get up at 4:30 in the morning so we could avoid the traffic heading into San Francisco. The drive took around an hour, and I slept the whole way, then kept myself entertained for the rest of the day by eating sandwiches, restocking shelves, and helping customers until 7:00 PM when we headed home.

I guess you could say that everything Baba knew about being a father came from his own experiences in Palestine. He put food on the table, supported us financially, and made sure we had everything we needed in life and in education. He even took me to the toy store damn near every week to buy me new toys. In that sense, I was totally spoiled. But he never showed any interest in how we were feeling emotionally. I mean, he didn't even know how to ask, "How are you?" or tell me that he loved me. I still haven't heard him say it till this day. I was twenty-one before I managed to tell my mama I loved her over the phone—and even then, I hung up immediately afterward so I wouldn't have to wait and see whether she said it back.

Mama cared for us emotionally, but there was only so much you were willing to share with a devout Muslim mother who you never wanted to disrespect. Unlike my father, she was deeply religious, which meant she often took me and my siblings to the mosque and tried to encourage us to pray five times a day. Sure, I sometimes lied and said I'd done it when I hadn't, but I never missed the evening prayer (Isha). I always felt that so long as I did my evening prayers, I was respecting my mama who, by this point, had managed to get herself an accounting degree along with being a housewife and taking care of us kids. She is a modern-day superwoman.

Of all my siblings, it was Noura I was closest to, possibly because we were birds of a feather. Above all, it was because she always let me be myself. I vividly remember running home from the kindergarten bus every day to make sure I caught the intro to the Tasmanian Devil show with her. I would jump onto her back as she leapt around the living room, dancing like no one was watching.

Still, I spent most of my time outdoors. Our neighborhood was a typical suburban area, and there was always someone to play with outside. I would sometimes ride my bike over to the park a few blocks away to play basketball, baseball, or mess around with paintball guns. I had the kind of childhood I thought everyone had—waking up and playing outdoors until the sun went down. I also assumed it would continue that way, right up until I started the first grade at Ardenwood Elementary School, and everything changed overnight.

Class was over for the day, and I was standing in the school-yard checking my bag to make sure I had all my books, when Nick (not his real name—even after all these years, I don't want to get into a confrontation with him) came over. Like me, he'd just started first grade, but he had a real thuggish character. You could tell he had older brothers and that they had taught him to act much older than he was. There was something about the look in his eyes too—when I met his gaze, I felt a chill inside.

"You have to buy me a gift," he said, launching a gob of spit onto the ground between us.

"What? Why?" I managed to stutter, though I could hear the uncertainty in my voice.

"Because it's my birthday tomorrow."

All evening that day, I paced anxiously back and forth on the ground floor of the house, waiting for Baba to get home. I kept checking the window to see if his car had pulled up outside, and when I finally saw him swing onto the driveway, I ran out to meet him.

Like always, Baba looked tired, but when he spotted me, I thought I could see a hint of a smile anyway.

"Baba!" I shouted. "Can we go to the toy store?"

"Now?" he asked, sounding surprised and running a hand through his thinning hair.

I explained that it was a school friend's birthday the next day and that I had to buy him a gift. If I had just been honest and told him the truth, the next few years would probably have been pretty different, but the problem was that I didn't know how to say any of that. All I knew was how easy it was to convince Baba to buy me things, and not long later, we were at Toys "R" Us across from NewPark Mall, which was a fifteen-minute drive from our place.

I remember I bought Nick five Tech Deck skateboards, wishing I was buying them for myself, and I also remember just how humiliating it felt to have to give them to him the next day. If I had been hoping it would convince him to leave me in peace, I was wrong; he took it as a sign that he could keep messing with me.

From that day on, I became Nick's bitch. I said everything he told me to say and did everything he told me to do—a fact that ultimately led to me being suspended from school for the first time.

It all started one lunch break in the third grade. Nick got into a fight with a bunch of sixth graders and made me fight alongside him. More accurately, he made me *start* the entire fight by throwing the first punch. I was so scared that my vision went blurry as I walked up to the kid Nick had told me to pick a fight with. Firstly, because I was so cautious and shy by nature, and secondly, because I had no idea how to fight. Besides, those kids were three years older than me. Somehow I managed to provoke the boy and punch him in the stomach, and next thing I knew the fight had started. It probably looked more funny than anything—a bunch of kids running around the yard, throwing punches at everyone and everything. Fortunately, a couple of teachers saw us and broke the whole thing up.

I ended up suspended for one week, Nick for two. But it made no difference in the long run because as soon as he came back, he kept on messing with me. The truth is, I was his errand boy right up to the seventh grade, when he transferred to another school. Thank goodness.

"I'm a true believer in Karma. You get what you give, whether it's bad or good."

—SANDRA BULLOCK

MISS CONGENIALITY

*Mama walks in on me jacking off,
and I begin a sexual relationship
with a family friend.*

As I mentioned earlier, Mama was a devout Muslim, but Baba wasn't particularly religious. That meant that whenever one of us kids slacked off praying, she took it out on him, convinced it was his fault. That wasn't the only thing they fought about, but it became a recurrent argument in the household.

I did my best to make my mama happy when it came to following my religion. I memorized a couple of surahs from the Quran, prayed when she asked me to and even fasted during Ramadan. To be honest, I actually enjoyed fasting because I was so skinny growing up I hated having to eat. So when Ramadan came around, not eating until sundown was a win for me.

Unlike Baba, my oldest brother, Mohammed, never missed a single prayer. After Mama, he was by far the most religious member of the family, and he would talk to me about Islam every single day, trying to make sure I prayed and didn't stray off the right path. Before I went to bed at night, he told me things like, "If you lose religion in your life, you're gonna lose yourself, and you're gonna end up alone. You may attain the world but you will be losing yourself."

He also told me that when he was going through school, he would have been lost and confused if it weren't for Islam, that everything would have been far messier. God provided him all the guidance and support he needed in life, he said. Considering he went to UCSD and then Harvard, I assumed it must have been true.

Mohammed was a whole decade older than me, so everything he said left a real impression. The only problem was that ever since I'd started the third grade, I had been growing increasingly curious in my sexuality. It didn't matter how hard I tried to shake off all lustful thoughts, they just kept coming back. Eventually, one day in the spring of 2001, the consequences of that would mess me up for life.

I had just gotten home from school when, like always, those thoughts started to take over. Around that time in my life, my classmates would talk about the porn they'd watched, but I still hadn't quite worked out exactly what that was. I guess that's why on this particular day I went straight up to my room, took off all my clothes, and put on *Miss Congeniality*, which was airing on TV.

I climbed on top of a life-sized toy leopard and started thrusting and humping while watching the movie, looking at myself in the mirror. I gripped my erect penis as I started to cum, but I got no further than that before the door to my bedroom opened and Mama stuck her head in.

All I remember is that I froze and felt completely blank. Mama seemed to feel something similar, because she just stood there, staring at me. "Get dressed now, Yousef!" she eventually yelled, slamming the door.

That evening, I wrote the following to her in an AOL email: *Mom, the devil got into my head…I apologize. I don't know what happened. I am still your son. It won't happen again.*

She replied a few hours later: *You let the devil get into your head. You have to pray, and you have to beat these feelings.*

That's all we ever said about it, which ensured that I carried a constant sense of guilt and shame around with me—a fear of feeling anything sexual. I was convinced it was the worst thing a person could do, and that it made me into a terrible person. It was the same when anything else happened in the family; we never had the emotional capacity to actually talk about how we felt. Instead, we sent emails or left notes for one another.

In any case, I started doing everything I could to stay away from all sexual thoughts and activity, and I actually managed it—at least for a while. To a large extent, it was because I was always so busy doing other stuff. I spent a load of time with the kids next door, roller blading, playing tennis, or terrorizing the neighborhood by TP-ing and egging houses and playing ding-dong ditch. We kept it up until we got caught. It happened one day while we were playing with our airsoft guns and one of us accidentally shot a grown-up neighbor in the back. He was so mad, he pulled out his phone and called the cops.

I don't think we'd ever run as fast as we did that day. We didn't stop until we reached the creek, which was at least ten blocks away, and we stayed there until dark, when one of us got hungry. Sadly, the minute we got back to our neighborhood, two cops were waiting for us.

One of them immediately decided I was the weakest link and pulled me to the side.

"I know you're the leader of the group," he said.

Looking back now, I know he was just trying to manipulate me because as he went on, he said: "I want you to tell me exactly what happened, then everyone goes home free." I was so scared I could barely breathe, so I just blurted out everything that happened in full detail.

Once the cops had gone, my friends wanted to know what they had asked and what I had told them. I couldn't tell them that I'd snitched, so I just said: "They asked what happened, and I said I didn't know, that I hadn't seen anything."

When our parents found out, some of them decided that we shouldn't hang out anymore. My parents didn't go that far, but

I do remember that they seemed concerned and disappointed (which was almost worse), and I wrote another email to my mama that evening, apologizing.

Around this time, we often used to visit relatives in San Francisco and the wider Bay area during the weekend. We'd go over to their houses to drink tea or eat dinner, and sometimes they'd come to visit us.

Despite that, the family we spent the most time with weren't relatives at all. They lived two blocks away and had a daughter around the same age as me. Her name was Emily, and my brother Ahmed (he's the middle one just older than me but younger than Noura) used to get us to act in his home movies. We filmed a video for the song "Macarena" and did a Princess Diana sketch, for example, and as soon as we were done, we would force our families to sit down in the living room and watch the finished product. I remember finding acting easy and loving the attention. Above all, I loved hanging out with Emily. I thought she was really pretty, and whenever we were alone, we'd run up to her room (if we were at her place) or mine (if we were at ours) and we would find ways to kiss or touch the way young children might. I always felt so guilty afterward, but I couldn't bring myself to stop, and when she and her family came over one evening that spring, Emily and I began play fighting on my bed. Tentatively at first, then increasingly wildly. Before long, I was on top of her, and I felt my erection pressing against her body. When I felt her move beneath me, I realized that I'd cum.

That was the starting shot in a long line of premature ejaculations and also the beginning of the double life I would go on to live as a Muslim-American.

"First loves can fuck you up."

—TARA KELLY

JUNIOR HIGH

The girl I'm secretly in love with shouts at me,
and I have to slow dance in front
of the entire school.

Starting junior high came as a real shock to me, partly because I was nowhere near as developed as most of the other students, but also because I was still incredibly shy and timid—just like I had been throughout elementary school.

On the first day back after summer break, I saw a boy and girl making out in the yard. Before long, one classmate after another started talking about how they'd lost their virginity, and though I tried my best to fit in and be cool, my insecurities and immaturity were constantly getting in the way. I guess the whole thing was made worse by the fact that I could constantly hear Mama's warnings and Muslim expectations echoing inside my head.

That's not to say that I didn't have a crush on anyone. I remember one girl in particular—every time I saw her, it was like my heart stopped, and I decided one day to tell a friend how I felt. I guess I did it hoping that he would pass it on to her, and when she started chasing me during lunch the next day, I remember thinking: *Yes, she likes me! She wants me!* At least I did until we'd run almost two laps of the school, and she caught up with me and pushed me up against a wall.

"Why are you going 'round telling people we're into each other?" she panted.

I just stared at her, confused, not knowing what to say.

"I don't like you," she said.

Her words felt like a punch to the gut, and I took a deep breath as she continued: "Stop talking about me!"

With that, she ran off.

Later that week, I found out that one of the teachers had nominated me to be the "Prince" at the upcoming ball, which meant I would have to suffer through a slow dance with some random girl while the rest of the school watched. This would be the first school dance I'd ever attended and the first time I'd ever dance.

I remember breaking out in a cold sweat when Mama took me to the mall to buy a suit, and when I tried it on in the bathroom the day of the dance, it was like it all became real. A wave of nausea rose up inside me, and next thing I knew I was on my knees in front of the toilet, throwing up.

Despite that, I forced myself to go to school the next evening, and as I walked into the gym hall, which had been transformed into an echoing disco, my legs felt like jelly. As though in a haze, and without looking at any of the other students, I went and sat down by myself by one of the walls.

The minutes that followed felt like the longest in my life, but then suddenly my teacher was on stage, announcing over the microphone that it was time for the Prince's dance.

I walked out onto the empty dance floor with the girl I was supposed to dance with a few steps behind. A ballad started thundering over the speakers.

I carefully took hold of her and started moving awkwardly in time with the music, closing my eyes and pretending I didn't exist.

When the song finally ended, I walked away without saying a word and sat back down by the wall. I sat there all evening, rubbing my sweaty palms together and staring blankly ahead.

"My dad always used to tell me that if they challenge you to an after-school fight, tell them you won't wait—you can kick their ass right now."

—CAMERON DIAZ

THE FIGHT

I get into my first real fight
and lose faith in true friendship.

You might think that the humiliation I'd already been forced to endure was enough, but unfortunately my life continued along the same tracks. As soon as I started high school, I kept getting into arguments with a guy called Dean in my Spanish class.

He responded by calling me all kinds of mean things, which I mostly ignored. But then one day he said something about my mama—something that went so far over the line I couldn't let it pass without looking weak.

Without really thinking about what I was doing, I got up and went over to his desk. The kid was smaller and weaker than me, which gave me a sense of bravery I usually didn't have.

"Repeat that if you dare," I told him. But before he had time to answer, I shoved his desk toward him so aggressively that he practically fell flat on his back.

Ordinarily, that would have been enough to start a fight, but since our teacher was nearby, we just shouted at each other and decided to settle things once school was over for the day.

The news spread like wildfire, and when people asked me whether it was really true, I said: "Yeah, we're gonna fight."

In truth, I wasn't really sure I wanted to. The anger I felt earlier had started to fade, and as I already mentioned, I didn't really know *how* to fight. But I had passed the point of no return, a fact I became painfully aware of as I stepped out into the yard and saw all the people who had stayed behind to watch. One of them was a girl who had a crush on me since elementary school. By this point the feeling was finally mutual, but one of my friends also had a crush on her, meaning I would never actually make a move out of respect. She and I were friends, though, and we used to walk home from school together. I saw her standing there with a half-proud, half-anxious look on her face, which made me—if possible—even more nervous. And when I heard someone shout "Go!" it was like all my strength drained out of my legs.

Somehow I managed to take a few steps toward Dean, fists raised. He had his fists clenched too, like a boxer. The only problem was that I had a sudden, powerful realization that I wouldn't be able to hit him in the face. Just the thought of it made me feel dizzy, so I started throwing punches at his body instead. Dean didn't seem to feel the same reluctance and quickly delivered blow after blow to my head.

It didn't take long for the first person to start laughing, and when I looked around me, I soon saw that everyone else had joined in.

"Come on, Yousef, you fight like a girl!" someone shouted.

"You scared of hurting his pretty face?" someone else yelled.

I knew I was making a fool of myself, but I just couldn't bring myself to do what everyone expected of me.

In desperation, I glanced over to my crush, and saw from her pained face just how embarrassed she was by the way I was mishandling the situation.

Right then, Dean caught me on the chin and everything went black. The fight was over.

Several of my friends came running over to ask why I wasn't fighting back. I mumbled something evasive and then peered over to the girl I had a crush on. I saw her look away and turn to leave with my friend—the one who also had a crush on her. From that day on, I started to withdraw. I still had friends, but they felt increasingly fake.

"In life we all go through trials
and tribulations.
So now tell me, will you pass
or will you make a mess?"

—JONATHAN ANTHONY BURKETT

MY FIRST GIRLFRIEND

I make my sexual debut,
and it marks me for life.

I got my first girlfriend by mistake. It all started when I developed a crush on a girl and started talking to one of her best friends, Eve. I guess I thought that Eve would be able to set us up somehow, but since I was so inexperienced and withdrawn, I didn't dare get straight to the point and cautiously asked what the girl I was interested in was like as a person instead. Eve was smart enough to know what was going on, but rather than laughing at me, she started giving me advice on how to get closer to her friend.

"She doesn't like cautious guys, so you need to be a bit more confident—but not too much, if you know what I mean."

I had no clue what she meant, but I nodded all the same, feeling like my window of opportunity was shrinking. I'd never managed to be particularly confident in approaching girls; I always got closer to them by joking or saying things that sounded weird as they came out. To be honest, I did consider myself weird. I always over analyzed situations, thoughts, and feelings. I could never just be "normal." Whatever that meant. Eve's advice was depressing because it proved that I didn't stand a chance.

Still, we kept talking during class breaks and after school, and she continued to give me advice that felt more or less impossible to put into practice. Maybe that was why we soon started talking about other things, and slowly but surely, I realized that I had a crush on Eve.

She was Filipino and super pretty, but what really appealed to me was her kindness and warmth, and I was shocked to find out that she had feelings for me too. So, after school one day, I summoned up all my courage and kissed her. Just a few days later, we were a couple.

That really was one of the happiest periods of my life, but I couldn't talk to my family about it. Mama and Mohammed in particular would never accept me having a girlfriend, so I kept Eve a secret and only took her home when I was sure no one else would be around.

By this point, all of my siblings had moved out, and Mama and Baba were both working throughout the day, so the set up worked pretty well. Or it did until Baba came home unexpectedly one day while we were making out in my bed.

I remember hearing his car pull up on the driveway and turning to Eve and saying: "Quick, you've gotta hide!"

I pointed to the closet.

She stared at me in disbelief.

"You've got to be kidding!"

"No, hurry up, Baba is coming!"

I more or less shoved Eve into my closet and closed the door on her.

My heart was pounding in my chest, and I barely dared breathe as I heard Baba come into the house and enter the kitchen. He started messing about with the coffee machine, and then I heard him start the microwave.

I thought about trying to smuggle Eve out of the house while he made a late lunch, but it felt far too risky. I was also worried Mama might come home and block the exit.

I was so deep in thought that I jumped when Eve started whispering irritably from inside the closet: "Can I come out now?"

"No, we've got to wait a little longer!" I whispered back, realizing just how absurd it was that I had to hide my girlfriend in my closet. I mean, this was California in the early 2000s.

To my relief, I heard Baba washing up not long later, then he left the house and started the engine. As soon as I saw him drive away, I let Eve out.

From that point on, we mostly met at her place or at the Jamba Juice on Mowry Avenue, not far from Fremont Hospital. We also spent a lot of time in my car, talking about anything and everything. In the end, there was no putting off the inevitable: sex.

I was almost eighteen and in my last year of high school, but I was still a virgin. Eve was too, which didn't feel like much of a consolation. Nor did it help my nerves when we drove my Honda Accord out to Coyote Hills one night in the fall to get the whole thing over and done with.

I remember gripping the wheel tight and trying to keep my breathing calm. Eve was probably nervous too because we didn't speak during the entire drive out there, and once I had parked up in the creepy park entrance, I couldn't concentrate on anything except the pitch black outside my car windows and the sound of the trees swaying from the wind outside.

Deep down, I think I was hoping Eve would say we should do it another time. But she just looked up at me like she really had made up her mind, and all I could do was start kissing her.

Not long later, we were in the back seat, and I felt a weird, pulsing dizziness as I fished a condom out of the pocket in my jeans and tried to put it on. I'd been struggling for some time when Eve said: "Do you want me to help you?"

"Uh…yeah."

Everything happened super fast after that. Eve managed to get the condom onto me without much trouble, but I came the minute I pushed inside her.

As though by reflex, I sat bolt upright with my hand on my crotch.

"What happened?" asked Eve.

I swallowed and stared out into the darkness at the knotty trees surrounding the parking lot, then licked my lips and said: "I came."

"Life is a bitch; you get used though,
or you kill yourself. Either way,
you're winning."

—AHMED MOSTAFA

MASSAGE PARLORS

*I do everything I can
to become a better lover.*

"I got a happy ending at a massage parlor yesterday."

I stared at my classmate as we walked home from school. "What's that?"

"You don't know?" he asked, laughing at me.

"Nah," I said. I honestly had no idea.

"It's when a masseuse ends the massage by giving you a hand job."

I stared at him in shock. "Wait, she did *that* for you?"

He nodded and grinned.

Still unsure whether to believe him or not, I managed to stutter: "How much did you pay?"

"Fifty bucks."

"Oh my god, that's insane."

I was quiet for a few seconds, then I asked: "Where is this place?"

It was spring, and my relationship with Eve was long over. Despite that, after everything that happened out in Coyote Hills, I still panicked at the thought of getting close to another girl, and maybe that's why, a few weeks later, I decided to look up the massage parlor my friend had mentioned. I thought that as I didn't know the women who worked there, I might be less nervous and get the chance to practice lasting longer.

I remember thinking that the people walking by on the sidewalk were looking at me with suspicion as I stepped inside, like they knew exactly why I was there and hated me for it.

In any case, I quickly made my way over to the woman behind the counter and tried my best to keep my voice steady as I said: "I'd like a one-hour massage."

"OK," she said with a shrug. "Follow me."

She led me through to a small room and told me to take off my clothes and lie down on the bed in the middle of the space.

I did as she said, and another woman came into the room. She told me to roll over onto my front, and as soon as I'd done that, she pulled my underwear down and spread a small towel over my ass. That act—it seemed like sheer routine to her—made me incredibly nervous. Instead of relaxing as she started to massage my shoulders and back with hands that felt both strong and soft, smelling like jasmine, I felt myself break out in a sweat.

"Just relax," she said, pressing harder on various places between my shoulder blades. After a while, since the massage seemed to be going like any other, I really did relax—until she told me to turn over. Because although she started by massaging my feet, she suddenly, and without warning, slapped my penis with her hand.

I remember tensing all over, assuming she must have hit it by mistake. But then she did the same thing again, and this time I had no choice but to open my eyes and meet her gaze. She looked straight at me and made a gesture that couldn't mean anything other than: Do you want a hand job?

I nodded and mumbled "Yes, please."

The woman smiled and removed the small towel before reaching for a bottle of massage oil. I realized just how hard I was and took a deep breath. It didn't help, because the minute the woman so much as *grazed* my penis, I came right over my stomach.

Her jaw dropped, but then she started laughing. Without uttering a single word, I got up from the bench, pulled on my clothes, handed her fifty bucks, and ran outside.

The shame I felt in that moment was indescribable. Ditto the anxiety that kept me awake all night. Despite all that, I couldn't help but go back to the same massage parlor the very next week— though I asked for a different masseuse. As it happened, that made no difference, and the whole thing ended in a sad repetition of my first visit.

Around the same time, during my last semester of high school, something happened that would change my life forever. I was on the way to my first class of the day one morning when the drama teacher caught up with me and said: "Yousef, I want you to audition for a play."

I just stared at him, because I had no real interest in the theater. I'd never even acted before, other than in the videos my brother Ahmed made of me and Emily. Besides, in those days I was playing on the high school football team, so I didn't have much free time. But the drama teacher went on: "I think you'd be a perfect fit, so I'm expecting you to come along to our audition!"

"When?" I asked, still feeling incredibly unsure.

"After school today, here's the script." He tossed it to me. "I want you to memorize this monologue. You'd be Einstein. Just do your best."

With that, he smiled and walked off.

I looked down at the script and didn't know what to think. The play was called *Picasso at the Lapin Agile*, which meant absolutely nothing to me. But the drama teacher had seemed so sure, and since I both liked and respected him, I spent lunch break that day learning the entire monologue.

I had no real idea how the audition went; I was so nervous I barely knew what I was doing. But when I got to school the next morning, several of my classmates came over and thumped me on the back, saying things like: "Congrats, Yousef!" and "Yeah, good job, man!"

I didn't know what they were talking about until I saw the noticeboard in the drama room. The teacher had cast me in the lead role, alongside Picasso, as Albert Einstein.

From that day on, I went to rehearsals every day and discovered, to my surprise, that not only did I think acting was cool, I actually seemed pretty good at it.

When the time came for the first performance, I invited all my friends including Eve. That was the night my dreams of becoming an actor really began.

"If you want to get laid, go to college.
If you want an education, go to the library."

—FRANK ZAPPA

SAN JOSÉ STATE
UNIVERSITY—COLLEGE

I lose myself.

"This is never going to work, Yousef." Mama said with a sigh. It was late summer 2008, and we were caught in traffic on the way to my first day of college orientation. I had somehow gotten accepted into San José State University. It was a pretty big shock to me since I was planning on going the community college route. Both were a let down from the standards my siblings had set. Mohammed in UCSD and Harvard. Noura, when she was at Berkeley Law School, and Ahmed in Berkeley as well pursuing becoming a pediatrician. "There's no way you'll be able to wake up early enough to make it to school on time." The original plan had been for me to live at home with Mama and Baba and commute to school, which was a thirty-minute drive from Fremont. But when Mama realized just how much traffic there was, she arranged for me to live in the nicest dorm on campus instead with some of my high school friends. How she always managed to find the money to help me when I was in need, I'll never know. But I always promised to pay her back.

One of the friends was André Quiazon, whom I shared a room with. Unlike me, André was very tidy and always folded his clothes carefully in the little closet. He kept his books in neat piles on his desk and never got fingerprints on the screen of his laptop.

He had the same routine every morning: he got up on time, made his bed, brushed his teeth and took a shower, got dressed in clean clothes (which he had also ironed), then shoved his laptop and a couple of books into his bag, and left in good time.

I, on the other hand, would roll out of bed in the same clothes I'd been wearing the day before and didn't have time to either wash or brush my teeth before I had to race off—only to arrive late on a regular basis.

That was my routine—until I got into a relationship with the hottest girl from my old high school—a girl I thought I'd never have a chance with. Her name was Amanda, and she was way out of my league, literally the sexiest woman I'd ever seen. Despite that, I heard on the grapevine that she was into me, and before long we started dating. The problem was that I was so afraid of having to repeat what I'd already been through—both with Eve in Coyote Hills and during my visits to various massage parlors—that I did everything I could to avoid having sex with her. But I was really attracted to her, and when she came back to my dorm one afternoon, I suddenly realized that I couldn't put it off any longer. Sadly, just like in Coyote Hills, we'd only just gotten started when I came.

I remember sitting on the edge of my bed, rubbing my clammy, cold hands together. I couldn't even meet Amanda's eye, and when the exact same thing happened again a few days later at her place, I just didn't know what to do.

I was spending virtually all my time thinking about it, and when the time came to go over to Amanda's place again, I decided I was going to have to talk to someone. I called my friend Abdullah and said: "Bro, I'm worried about having sex, and I'm worried about cumming too fast. What should I do?"

There was a moment's silence on the other end of the line, lasting way too long to be comfortable. But then I heard Abdullah say: "Just do what I do…. Once you start, rap out a song in your head. It'll help."

A few hours later, when Amanda and I tried to have sex again, I chose the song "A Milli" by Lil Wayne—purely because it's pretty long. As I pushed into her, I was reciting the words as slowly as I could in my head, starting with *A milli*.... *A milli*.... *A milli*.... Sadly, I didn't even make it to "a millionaire" before I was done. I knew right there and then that there was something seriously wrong with me, but I had no idea what to do about it—even less what I was supposed to say to Amanda, who got up to take a shower and then came back to give me another chance. So, again, I tried to rap along with "A Milli" in my head, and yet again I got no further than "a millionaire" before I came.

I realized that the fact I came so quickly would ruin my future prospects—not just with Amanda but with any other girlfriends I might have. Those fears were confirmed a few weeks later, at a New Year's Eve party, when I spotted Amanda making out with her ex.

That was the starting shot in a really unhealthy period of self-hate and junk food. I ended up putting on so much weight that the skinny, good-looking boy I'd been in high school disappeared. I also started drinking and smoking weed with my friends, and I joined a fraternity—Delta Upsilon—which largely involved partying. But while my friends managed to stay on top of it, I let go completely and saw no point to making an effort at school. Which meant I got a 0.67 GPA my first semester of college.

I became increasingly blue and introverted, which also made it harder for me to relate to my friends. It felt like they were a different species. Maybe that was why, one afternoon at the start of that very first term, I hurried back to my room after class, pulled out my laptop, and started writing what would eventually become a whole bunch of spoken word poetry. Before the fall term was over, I read them to an audience at a spoken word event in a café on campus.

Aside from that, my work wasn't up to much. In truth, I flunked almost every single class after falling asleep during a written test (among other things) and was soon on the brink of being kicked out. In order to stay enrolled, I had to take a remedial math exam, but since math was one of my worst subjects, I felt like I had no choice but to ask one of my friends for help.

"You have to take that test for me," I said, quickly adding, "Please, I'll pay you."

Two days later, he took the test, and since no one found out, I continued that way all spring term—paying friends to take exams and do course work for me.

"I feel sorry for every Therapist, Psychologist, and Psychiatrist I've ever met. I know I've put thoughts in their mind they will never forget."

—STANLEY VICTOR PASKAVICH

BIPOLAR

I lie to Mama and have a breakdown in the library.

One day in the early summer of 2009, Mama called to see how I was doing. It was something she often did, but that day stuck in my memory because when I told her I was doing great, I realized for the first time just how easy it was to lie to her. Sure, I'd done the same just a few months earlier when I told her I was studying Business Marketing at college—in actual fact, I had switched to a Theater Arts major during the very first week—but it felt different this time.

The truth was that ever since I moved to San José, I'd been struggling with increasingly dark and destructive thoughts, to the extent that I often found myself fantasizing about taking my own life. Looking back now, I can see that this was a consequence of the double life I'd been living with all the drinking and smoking and visits to massage parlors, plus the guilt I felt whenever I thought about Mama and Baba and how they would feel if they knew what I was really like as a person. Not that I was seriously planning on killing myself, but the fantasies refused to go away, and they made it hard for me to focus on anything else.

Maybe that was why I took my laptop to the library with me one day in an attempt to study. Sadly, it didn't help.

At first, it was the complete silence that bothered me, but then I noticed the rows of students sitting at their tiny desks, working away on their computers like the living dead.

I found an empty chair and opened my laptop on the desk in front of me, bringing up the paper I was supposed to submit the very next day. But the minute I tried to get to work, it was like the words kept drifting away from me, and before long I was lost in thought about disappearing in one way or another—ideally for good. I felt my heart racing in my chest, and I broke out in a cold sweat. Next thing I knew, I could hear the sound of my own heavy breathing and saw the students around me glancing over—which only made me breathe even harder.

Panicking, I closed the computer and shoved it into my bag, then hurried out of the library and ran miles to the Delta Upsilon frat house where my school friends and I had moved. The tears started flowing down my cheeks as I ran, and when I finally got to my room, I was relieved to see that none of my three roommates were home. I almost never got any time to myself there—particularly not at night, when I often had to pull the covers up over my head so I wouldn't hear whatever they were doing with their girlfriends or other girls who were staying over.

I threw myself onto the bunk bed and kept asking what was going on. I felt my stomach churning, a dull pain spreading across my chest, right out into my arms. Every breath was a struggle, and I realized I needed help.

I called the hospital—Kaiser Permanente in Fremont—and was put through to the emergency psych ward.

A woman answered, and I heard how desperate I sounded as I panted, "Something's wrong with me...seriously wrong."

The woman remained calm as she asked me about my symptoms and told me to talk her through what happened. She said, "I think you should see a psychologist," and gave me an appointment a few days later.

Because I no longer felt like I could trust myself, the wait for that appointment was unbearable, and by the time I finally drove over to the hospital, I was so exhausted from all the tension that I could hardly keep my eyes open as I sat down in the waiting room.

Because I had no experience with psychology or therapy, I didn't know what to expect, and as I sat there, I found myself thinking about how Mama and Baba would react if they found out what their youngest son was up to.

"Yousef Erakat?"

I looked up and saw a middle-aged man with a neat beard smiling at me.

I followed him through to a sparsely furnished room, and he told me to sit down in an armchair. He took a seat opposite me and picked up a notebook from the side table.

"I'd like you to tell me why you're here today," he said.

I don't know if it was his calm, steady gaze that made me open up, but I found myself giving him a detailed description of what I'd been going through lately, and by the time I was done he looked up from his pad and said, "Could you give me an example of what these suicidal thoughts are like?"

I took a deep breath. "Sometimes, when I'm driving my car, I imagine what would happen if I just turned the steering wheel all the way to the left. Then it would all be over."

He wrote something in his pad, and I heard just how anxious I sounded when I asked, "Is it OK to have that kind of thought? I never thought I'd actually kill myself."

He looked up at me with a warm smile. "I believe you, and you're not alone in having these thoughts. But what is concerning is that they're taking up so much of your mental capacity. I'm going to give you another appointment for next week, so we can try to work out a way to help you."

As I drove away from the hospital that day, I felt completely drained, and for the first time in a long while, I had no trouble at all sleeping that night.

Over the days that followed, however, the wait to continue the conversation with the psychologist felt never-ending again. I was just hoping he could help me escape the nightmare I was living in.

At the same time, I felt anxious as I drove back to the hospital at the end of that week, because I didn't know what might come up during our next conversation.

But somehow, he managed to get me to relax as I sat there in his consulting room, and when our session was almost over, he said: "I think we've made progress today, but we probably need another session."

I didn't know if I should feel relieved or disappointed, because obviously I wanted to get treated as quickly as possible. But I also wanted the chance to talk properly about my problems, so that the treatment could be properly effective.

"I think I know what you're suffering from," the psychologist said as I sat down in his chair for the fifth or sixth time.

"Oh yeah?" I asked, feeling a sudden dizzy sensation.

"You might be manic depressive—or bipolar as it's known these days."

He must have been able to see how scared I was because he quickly added, "But there are some great medicines available, and we'll try to find something that works for you."

"We're all pretty bizarre. Some of us are just better at hiding it, that's all."

—*THE BREAKFAST CLUB*

TRUST ISSUES

I fall in love with a pathological liar
and lose all my hair.

Did the many long talks I had with the psychologist make me happier? The truth is that they helped me as little as the medication, which simply made me put on weight and lose a load of hair. When I had told my mama about being diagnosed with having bipolar and severe depression she began to cry. Apparently it's a thing on my dad's side of the family and she believed I could overcome it without pills through the power of prayer and belief in religion.

As if that wasn't bad enough, my issues with girls had also become much worse since I moved into the frat house. Life there revolved around the special brotherhood between the guys, but I'd never quite found my way in.

Sure, I liked drinking and partying with them, but since the conversation inevitably came 'round to sex, I always found myself on the outside. Talking about my issues with premature ejaculation simply didn't feel like the right way to become one of the guys.

It also proved to be an issue in my relationships with girls, making me even more withdrawn than I had been in high school. Despite that, I started dating a girl from my college, and the simple fact that she seemed to want me was so overwhelming that I immediately put her up on a pedestal and went on and on about how much I loved and needed her. All my previous unrequited love had left such a mark on me that I literally clung onto her.

I also tormented her with confessions about my inner darkness, and looking back now, I can't work out what must have scared her most. All I know is that one day she turned to me and said she didn't want to date me anymore.

"Why not?" I asked, completely taken aback. But later that evening, when I told Brandon, one of my friends from the frat house, what had happened, he just sighed and said: "You gave her way too much attention and love."

"How is it possible to give someone too much attention and love?" I asked, adding, "Surely I can show the person I'm dating that I love them?"

"Yeah, but if you keep showing it constantly, going on and on about it, she's gonna get sick of you. From now on, you're not gonna pick up when she calls, and you're not gonna reply to her texts. Ignore her completely and see what happens."

I reluctantly agreed to do as he said, despite every single instinct telling me to pick up the minute I saw her name on my phone screen. By the end of that week, she came up to my room in the frat house. With tears in her eyes, she said, "I'm so sorry for everything I did. I want you back."

It was like the ground swayed beneath my feet. Because at that moment (probably because I was young and inexperienced) I got the sense that what makes a girl respect you and want you was rationing your feelings—and sometimes even ignoring them.

"Oh yeah?" I said to her. Right there and then, as that insight struck me, I lost all interest not just in her, but in girls in general.

At the same time, thanks to the relentless force that affects all young, heterosexual guys, I was still drawn to girls. Before long, I actually developed a crush on a girl in my Asian-American Studies class, and after lusting after her from a distance for a while, I summoned up all my courage and wrote a note to her one day. "Meet me downstairs in five minutes."

The girl, who had dark hair and brown almond shaped eyes, smiled in reply. I told the teacher I had to go to the dentist, then left the room and went down to the lobby to wait for her.

A few minutes later, I saw her coming down the stairs, and before she even had time to walk over to me, I'd practically dreamed up an entire relationship.

We walked out to my car in the parking lot, and I was happy to discover that she was really easy to talk to. The fact that she was hot was something I tried to ignore because I knew I would never be able to sleep with her, even if that opportunity opened up.

Either way, we started hanging out, and after a while she turned to me and said, "Just so you know, I have a boyfriend."

We were standing in the parking lot outside school at the time, and I had to make a real effort to hide how disappointed I felt. At the same time, I didn't know how to interpret the pained look on her face.

"He's really abusive," she explained.

For a moment, neither of us spoke, but then I said, "So why don't you leave him?"

She stared down at the ground and swallowed.

"Because he lets me live with him, and I don't have any place else to go."

I remember smiling as I said, "You know you can stay with me."

Just a few days earlier, my friends and I had moved into a house down the street from the frat house, and when I got back later that afternoon, I gathered the guys in the kitchen to explain the situation. No one spoke for a few seconds, then one of them said, "You're bringing a girl here?"

"Yeah, she has nowhere else to go," I said, trying to ignore his grin when I awkwardly explained that she was just a friend.

The truth is that I really did treat her like a friend. I didn't so much as touch her as she lay in bed beside me those next few nights, telling me how afraid she was that her boyfriend would find her and what he might do if he did.

In those moments, it felt strange not to know what I was most afraid of: her boyfriend finding us, or—in case she suddenly pressed herself against me—her finding out just how lousy a lover I was.

But though we were never intimate with each other, she still managed to get under my skin and always got me to do whatever she wanted. One day, for example, when she got a part time job as a waitress, she told me, "But the café is downtown, and I don't have a car."

"You can borrow mine," I said, without even pausing to think. By that point, I was hopelessly in love with her, and any idiot could have seen that and knew she was exploiting that fact.

A few days later, she called me from the car, but I barely had time to open my mouth before she started ranting about an argument she had gotten into at her new job. I heard her scream, and next thing I knew, there was a loud bang.

"What's going on?" I shouted.

"I crashed!"

"Are you hurt?"

She wasn't, but the damage to my car was far more than I could afford.

A few weeks later, I got a call from a number I didn't recognize, and when I picked up, I heard a man's voice. He told me he was her boyfriend, and as I tried to compose myself, he continued, "Do you remember the car accident she was in?"

"Yeah."

"I was in the car with her."

"Oh," I said, swallowing.

"Another thing you should know: every night, before she goes over to your place, she has sex with me. She's playing you, man."

I took a deep breath, feeling resigned, and asked, "Why?"

"Well," the guy laughed, "you better ask *her*."

But I never did, I just told her not to come over to my place again.

Around the same time I found out that my first ex (Eve) had been sleeping with one of my best friends during the time we were together because I was so bad in bed. The whole thing made me lose all faith in humanity, but, more than anything, it made me lose faith in myself.

"For an idea that does not first seem insane, there is no hope."

—ALBERT EINSTEIN

THE KNOCKOUT

I get blind drunk and have a brilliant idea.

By this point, I could neither trust girls nor touch them, but in the fall of 2010, I started dating someone new, named Alice. I know you're probably wondering, why keep dating girls? My inability to sexually connect left an emotional hole inside of me that I was hoping someone would be able to fill. Before long, she started asking questions about why I was so elusive. She also wanted to know why I kept my clothes on when we lay side by side in bed at night. I didn't know how to explain any of it to her, and the more frustrated she got, the more performance anxiety I felt—not least because all I wanted to do was impress her.

That might help explain what happened one night just before Christmas. My fraternity, Delta Upsilon, was throwing a huge party, and for several days beforehand, I was nervous because I knew Alice was coming and had told me she wanted to finally have sex that night. I ended up drinking far too much, and now have only a few memories of that evening—laughing far too loud, my girlfriend's angry face, a glass table being knocked over—before everything goes black.

When I came 'round, I had no idea where I was. I squinted up at the bright sunlight filtering in through the blinds and noticed there was a plastic hospital bracelet around my wrist. I soon noticed other details, and they worried me. A hospital would never allow pictures of centerfold girls on the walls, for example. Next thing I knew, the door opened and one of my friends came in.

"Where am I?" I heard myself slur.

"In my bed."

Right then, I felt the pain in my head spread through my whole body, and I had to lick my lips before I could ask: "What happened?"

"You got punched in the face by some football players. Go back to sleep."

But I couldn't, of course. I needed to know what I'd done, in detail, and my friend patiently explained that I got so drunk that when everyone started to head home, I stood in the doorway with my arm outstretched, stopping them from leaving.

"I think you were trying to impress Alice," he said. "You just stood there with this big grin on your face, saying 'If you wanna go, you'll have to limbo under my arm.' The only problem was that two big guys from the football team showed up, and one of them said, 'You have three seconds to get out of the way before I punch you in the face. One, two....' Then he got you with a right hook. You basically lifted up off the ground and landed on your back. You hit your head so hard you passed out, so we called an ambulance and they took you to the hospital. You woke up there but were still totally out of it. Either way, it doesn't look like you have any brain damage."

I took a deep breath and picked up my phone. Just as I'd feared, my entire Facebook page was full of people saying, "Get well soon," "Hope you feel better," "I'm so sorry," and "Wish it didn't happen to you."

I realized that the whole campus must be talking about what had happened, so I packed up my things and moved back home with Mama and Baba the very next day.

Strangely enough, it didn't feel like a defeat. It actually felt liberating to return to my boyhood room. I started taking care of myself in a way I hadn't while I was living on campus, watching what I ate and regularly working out. After just a few months, I'd lost all the weight I gained from drinking and eating so much in college and got into the best shape of my life thanks to an at home workout program called P90X. This is also when I started practicing using the law of attraction before even knowing what it was. Before I began to lose weight, I emailed the creators of P90X called Beach Body and told them that they should have me on their infomercial. I got a reply back stating that it didn't work like that and I first had to lose the weight, send in my results to even be considered. So I did exactly that. Put the intention of being in the infomercial in my head. And sure enough, three months later, my application was accepted and I was soon on a TV infomercial.

I'm convinced that all this played a part in the idea that popped into my head one morning that refused to go away.

One day when I was having lunch with two girlfriends they had told me that it was time I started my own YouTube channel since in the past all I did was star in Qias Omars videos. I'd been involved in a few sketches on Qias Omar's channel in high school, but it was just for fun and nothing I'd ever considered as a possible path for myself. It was a lot of fun and taught me a lot about YouTube and I owe a huge portion of the inspiration to start thanks to Qias. YouTube was still relatively new at the time, and I had a clear idea of how I could start a channel that really stuck out. I started sketching out the kind of things I'd like to feature on my channel that very same afternoon. I even came up with a name that played on the letters of my name. fouseyTUBE. Just reverse the Y and the F of Yousef. And it's not YouTube, because it's MY Tube so fouseyTUBE. Get it?

A few days later, I had prepared a presentation and hoped to show it to someone. I didn't know any sponsors or anything like that, so the people I picked as my test pilots were a friend and one of my cousins. If they liked the idea, I hoped I'd be able to convince them to join me because I didn't want to do the channel all on my own. That night, I called them both and invited them to meet me at a pizza shop near San José State.

Both my cousin and my friend were already waiting when I arrived.

"What's with the whiteboard?" my cousin asked me, pointing to the board beneath my arm.

"It's so you understand just how fucking cool this is," I said, ordering a cola and a slice.

"What?" asked my friend.

"My idea for a YouTube channel."

They stared at each other, looking unsure—the way people look when they think someone might have lost their mind.

But I didn't care, I just put up my board and started drawing on it as I explained my idea.

"We're gonna create viral videos on a regular basis, and we're gonna target the Middle Eastern Muslims around the world through comedy."

But in truth, I didn't know a thing; I was just going off intuition and gut feeling. And judging by their faces, their intuition and gut feelings were telling them something completely different.

When I woke up the next morning, I went straight down to Mama in the kitchen. I told her: "Mama, I love you and never ask for much (all though to be fair growing up I asked for a lot and she never said no), but I have an idea for a YouTube channel and need a camera and a laptop. I promise to pay you back for everything. But please help me now."

Mama agreed to help me with the purchase but made me promise her then and there that this would only be a hobby and that no matter what I would finish my studies and graduate from college. I went to Best Buy the very next day to buy my first camera and laptop.

"Can you imagine if social media websites were people and just how fucked up those people would be?"

—TROYE SIVAN

FOUSEYTUBE

I poke fun at my family and culture,
and people love me for it.

Around this time, the guy who had been nominated as best actor in the previous year in my Theater Arts department group came to class to talk about his life after college. I was sure he must be making Hollywood movies or at least performing in a stage musical somewhere, but when the moderator asked what he was doing now, he said, "I'm working at a restaurant and going to auditions." It was then that I realized that being a Theater Arts major was never going to be enough to make me an actor. I would have to create opportunities for myself and knew that a YouTube channel would be the perfect platform. I could use everything I'd learned in class to perform sketches and, little by little, get better at what I was doing.

"Well, thank you for coming in to talk about your career," I heard the moderator say.

What career? I thought, watching as the guy put back the microphone with a look on his face that clearly revealed just how much he was suffering at having to broadcast his failure to the class.

Personally, I felt more convinced than ever that I'd discovered a way forward that could work for me, and on March 25, 2011, I launched fouseyTUBE with my very first video—"Rebecca Black Dancing In the Apple Store to Friday."

At the time, there was this craze for going into Apple stores, dancing in front of all the unsuspecting customers, and filming their reactions. I had absolutely zero nerves or shame because I was convinced this was my path to fame. I also knew that I needed to go viral if I wanted to gain any followers at all, so I made every video with that specific intention. After just a few months, I managed it for the very first time.

It was two in the morning, and I was lying awake in bed when a sudden thought crept into my head: I could play all the characters, acting out what it was like to live in a Middle Eastern household. Just like Tyler Perry did in his movies. I would be the mom, dad, grandma, sister, and any other members of the family.

When I got up the next morning, I called a friend of mine and said, "I need help recording something, can you come over?"

Thirty minutes later, he was at my place. By then I had set up the camera, and I told him to wait next to it while I ran upstairs and raided my parents' closet. I grabbed some of Mama's headscarves and one of her Palestinian dressing gowns. I put everything on and went back down to my friend, who got up to leave the minute he saw me.

"No, please, hold on. I got this," I said.

But in all honesty, I had no script, no lines; I was running on intuition and a whole bunch of memories from childhood—stuff I'd picked up from listening to my relatives during family gatherings.

I stared at my friend and said, "Press record." He sighed but did as I said, and I immediately started impersonating my mama. It was like a spirit had taken over me, and I was going from scene to scene, changing locations and settings. When I was done, I changed into Baba's clothes and recreated the exact same scenes, only with Baba's responses this time.

Once I was done with him, I dressed up as my usual self, responding to everything I'd said as both Mama and Baba, even matching the eye line to exactly where I was sitting as my parents.

Later that night, I went onto YouTube and started searching for information on how to edit a video. Everything I'd done so far had been uploaded pretty much how it was shot using iMovie, but I needed to edit the different takes together. After watching a bunch of videos, I downloaded Final Cut Pro and started trying out different things, eventually producing a video I titled "Middle Eastern Parents." I did not go to sleep that night. I knew I had a viral video on my hands and was super anxious to upload it that next morning. It was like an intuition in my gut telling me that this video would spread like wild fire.

Within just a few days, I had more views than I ever could have hoped for. The video amassed a giant audience and was being shared over all social medias at the time, primarily Facebook. I was so hungry and determined for success I would create Events on Facebook and invite every single friend I had to attend the virtual premiere for a new video of mine. I would also open every single chat on my Facebook and copy and paste the link. I was willing to do anything and everything to make sure I was successful in my vision.

Feeling inspired, I kept making new videos, releasing them week after week. I gave them names like "The Hummus Dance" and "Middle Eastern Mistakes." I even made a full-on series called "Middle Eastern Family," and I'll never forget the day I showed the first part to Mama. It was late afternoon, and she was standing by the stove like always when I came into the kitchen with my laptop.

"Come look at this, Mama," I said as I put my computer on the table.

She sat down in one of the chairs with a blank face. I hit play on the first video, and once it was over she kept staring straight ahead, not saying a word. Eventually she mumbled a little and then said, "How did you get us so spot on? How do you know how we say things? How do you know how we act?"

She looked up at me.

"I didn't know you were so talented."

Though Mama was upset when I told her about having switched to Theater Arts instead of Business Marketing, she had at least always taken my interest in theater seriously; she had come to every single show I was in. Around this time, I was in a play in which I kissed two girls and had an implied sexual relationship with one of them. Afterward, Mama turned to me and said, "Yousef, this is what I'm scared of if you ever make it to Hollywood. You're going to have to do things that are against our religion." If only she knew what I was already doing that was against our religion.

At the time, I just smiled at her, but I've often returned to that moment since.

One day in Fremont when I was running errands a girl came up to me in the grocery store a few blocks from our house. She was a couple years older than me, and I'd never seen her before, so at first I didn't know what she wanted.

"Hey, I saw you on YouTube," she told me. "You're great! Can I take a picture?"

For a moment, I thought she was just messing with me, but she already had her phone in her hand and was giving me this real pleading look, so I told her, "Sure."

It was the most exhilarating feeling I'd ever had because I realized just how big my videos were becoming. It was like I finally understood that there were real people behind all the views.

But as more and more people started watching me, I also started getting mean comments beneath my videos—so mean that just a few months after I first launched, I had my first mental breakdown. The negative comments came from people who felt like I was disrespecting my culture and religion by poking fun at them in my videos. A lot of people were also just envious of my success. Telling me that I would never succeed and that my career would soon be over.

I couldn't understand why people who didn't know me wanted me to suffer. The fact I was on my way into a deep depression at the time obviously didn't help.

On top of that, the dean of my department called me in to her office one day. At first, I assumed she just wanted to congratulate me on my success, but once the small talk was out of the way, she turned serious and said, "I do feel like I should warn you that this channel 'fawseyTUBE' or whatever it's called, could turn out to be the biggest mistake you ever make in your acting career."

I stared at her, confused. "What do you mean?"

"I don't think anyone in Hollywood will take you seriously if you continue with this...stuff."

It was obvious she thought my YouTube sketches were silly. I actually got the sense she thought I was embarrassing the entire university.

She wasn't the only one who thought I was lame. I remember, for example, walking past the green room where the acting students hung out one day. "Did you see Yousef's latest YouTube video?" someone inside asked. "Ha ha, he actually thinks this is going to get him somewhere." Everyone in the room started laughing.

Another time, I asked one of my Theater Arts professors if I could show one of my YouTube sketches while we were sharing the projects we were working on, but they just gave me a patronizing glance and said, "No, we only show real art in this classroom."

Still, plenty of other people seemed to appreciate my videos, and I got offers to appear in a lot of different cities, not just in the USA, but also abroad. For instance, I got invited to headline a big comedy festival in Sydney and flew out there with Mama. In those days I was managing myself and wasn't sure what fee to ask for, so I just asked for the cost of the plane tickets and another $500. When I walked out on stage that night and saw the audience—3,500 people—I realized that I'd sold myself too cheaply.

At the time I wasn't making much money off of YouTube itself. I had produced viral after viral hits and even one video that got noticed on MTV and VH1's websites, "Shit Drake Says." Despite that, at the end of each month I rarely received more than around $300. I thought this was totally normal and I would have to work harder to make more money. Money wasn't my intention while I was chasing fame so I didn't mind it much. It was only when my manager at the time linked me with a YouTube network called Fullscreen that I found out what was really happening.

When I first started YouTube I signed to a YouTube Network that I had received an email from and they were doing my pay outs. In actuality the network was run by a single man in his garage. Over the course of a year he pocketed over $250,000 from me sending me $300 each month. Once I had signed with Fullscreen my manager had called me while I was in a layover from one of my comedy shows and shared some big news with me. "Fullscreen just sent you your first payment for the month. $25,000." I instantly began to shake and cry. I hung up and called my mom and told her she would never have to work again. I had finally felt like I made it.

Either way, getting back to San José State and my life as a student after a gig was a pretty massive contrast, to put it mildly.

All in all, I felt less motivated than ever to get to grips with my terrible grades. As the end of my final semester approached, I realized that I wasn't going to manage to complete two classes— meaning I wouldn't be able to receive my diploma.

As far as I was concerned, it didn't really matter, but I knew Mama would see it as a failure, and not just for me but for the entire family. So I went to the administrative office and asked if there was any way I could complete the two classes over summer and still get my diploma and walk across the stage during graduation. They said that was fine, so I signed up secretly to those two summer classes—knowing full well that I wouldn't attend them. But at least that meant I could attend graduation and walk across the stage. That day will forever be one of my greatest accomplishments in life. The smile and cheers I received from my mama were worth more than anything YouTube could have given me. The dean of the department also showed up on stage to announce the winner of Actor of the Year, and although I'd been in every college play over the previous two years, I'll never forget how surprised I was that she seemed to have suddenly changed her attitude toward me. She said: "Some of our students make their own ways in their career through the internet.... I'm so happy to award Actor of the Year to one of the most talented students we've ever had here at San José State. I've always supported him in his vision and what he is doing. I'm so proud of him, and I want to congratulate Yousef Erakat, aka Fousey."

"Los Angeles, give me some of you!
Los Angeles come to me the way I came to
you, my feet over your streets, you pretty
town I loved you so much, you sad flower
in the sand, you pretty town."

—JOHN FANTE

MOVING TO LA

Without knowing it, I go through my first long-term depression.

As soon as Mama and I got home from the graduation cere-mony, I sat down in front of the computer in my room and started searching Craigslist for an apartment in LA. I think I called the very first one I found, and when I asked the guy if it was still available, he said: "Yeah...but a whole bunch of people have already called about it."

"If I come tomorrow, can I have it?"

"Sure," he said.

So, the very next day, I hopped on a plane to Los Angeles. I went to view the place and signed my very first lease despite barely even knowing what a lease was. I flew back that night like nothing had happened.

I didn't tell my family any of this, not until the end of the month when, after dinner one day, I started packing my things. I remember Mama popped her head round the door as I was filling a huge box of clothes.

"What are you doing?" she asked.

"I'm moving."

"Where?"

As the word "LA" left my mouth, she started crying, and looking back now, I can understand why. The whole time I was in college, I'd been telling her that I wouldn't move up there until I graduated—just for her sake—but I think she'd tried to put off the knowledge that eventually I'd be leaving, because she was so scared. I mean, I was the last of her children still at home, and I'd also chosen a pretty uncertain path for myself (my older siblings had, by that point, all become doctors or lawyers).

Baba didn't react to my news in the same way at all. He didn't even give me a proper hug as I packed up my things and did one last loop of the house to check that I hadn't missed anything. Not that he wasn't sad or feeling anything, he just didn't know how to emotionally connect with me.

I was terrified, and from the moment I left Fremont, I cried non-stop for the eight hours it took to drive to LA Because although I was doing exactly what I wanted—something I had been dreaming of for years—it all just felt so sudden. If I hadn't had J. Cole's "Friday Night Lights" mixtape on repeat, I probably wouldn't have found the strength to keep going; I would've made a U-turn and driven straight back home. The intro to the mixtape still mirrors in my head on a daily basis.

My new apartment was on Barrington Avenue, and I'll never forget stepping into the unfurnished space late that night, breathing in the musty air.

As far as I can remember, I didn't even take my things inside; I just curled up on the hard wood floor and went to sleep.

While I was living with my parents, I rarely gave much thought to my mental health, but now that I was suddenly all alone, I realized for the first time just how sick and depressed I really was.

I spent over a week doing nothing but sitting on the floor of my new apartment by myself, drenched in cold sweat, as two thoughts swirled round my head: *What am I doing here?* And *why do I feel this way?*

In order to numb the anxiety that felt like it was going to drive me crazy, every night I went to the liquor store right across the street to buy a twelve pack of Blue Moon beer. I drank until I passed out, and whenever I had to eat, there was a Subway just downstairs.

Whenever my parents called—which they did every day—to see how I was and how things were going, I lied as not to worry them and told them I was feeling great and that everything was going fine. I pretended I had meetings and auditions every day, and that I was making one video after the other. All so that they wouldn't realize how lost and confused I was.

**"My body is my journal,
and my tattoos are my story."**

—JOHNNY DEPP

TATTOOS

I try to rebel against my religious upbringing but regret it almost immediately.

After spending countless months alone in my apartment, I eventually started to force myself to get out and about. The area where I lived might not have been the best, but if I took the car, it only took me thirty minutes to get to Santa Monica.

At around the same time, I also started taking acting classes. The problem was that I wasn't doing well, and I was living the kind of life Mama could never have imagined—even in her wildest dreams. That meant I constantly felt torn, and one afternoon while I was sitting in acting class I felt a sudden urge to get a tattoo. I got up and ran out to my car, then drove straight to the first tattoo parlor I could find in Venice Beach.

Since I didn't think the medication I was taking for my bipolar disorder was helping, I'd started self-medicating, and on that particular day I'd smoked so much weed that any thought of consequences went straight out of the window. After parking up on the street outside, I went into the tattoo parlor, pointed to my right forearm and said: "I want you to write 'fouseyTUBE' here."

"OK," the tattooist said, laughing.

I followed him through to a back room and sat down in what looked like a dentist's chair.

The main reason I wanted a tattoo was probably because it was the worst thing I could do in my mother's eyes, and therefore the ultimate sign of emancipation. I mean, I'd been able to hide my smoking and drinking and even the girls I'd dated, but a tattoo was impossible to cover up. Besides, all the guys in LA seemed to have tattoos, and I wanted nothing more than to fit in.

I was living a complete double life. Here I was online presenting myself as a straight edge devout Muslim boy making people laugh and helping them feel inspired. But in reality, I was a fraud. If they knew who I really was deep down, they would despise me. I mean, drinking, smoking, having premarital sex, going to massage parlors to escape reality? Who on earth was I?

One minute I was sweating in the chair, the next I was freezing, but I just wanted to get it over and done with. For the first time in my life, I felt like I was the one making the decisions.

The next day, I felt so liberated when I looked down at my tattoo that I immediately decided to get another. Much bigger this time.

I drove over to a tattoo parlor on Melrose and told the tattooist to write J. Cole's slogan "A Dollar and a Dream" on my right forearm, directly beneath my first tattoo.

Sadly, the minute I got home I regretted the whole thing. I suddenly found myself thinking not just about Mama and my grandmother, but all the millions of disappointed Muslim fans I would have if they found out. Right there and then, it felt like my entire career was over, and I started to hyperventilate and began to cry.

I kicked off my shoes and walked round and round my apartment, heart racing in my chest with a metallic taste in my mouth. Then, though I didn't really know why, I sat down at the computer and wrote the following words to my mama:

I'm so sorry for all the times I went against what you wanted me to do. I apologize. I love you. I'm still your son.

Yousef

As soon as I had sent the email, I went straight into the bathroom and jumped into the tub. I spent two hours scrubbing the tattoos, crying and praying they would wash off.

Though the tattoos represented everything I wanted to be, they also represented everything my mama and my Muslim fans hated. The hot water wasn't enough to remove them, of course, and I started to worry that I might have ruined them in the process. I decided to head back to the parlor on Melrose, and when I got there the next morning, I said to the guy: "Hey man, could you check my tattoo to see if I messed it up?"

He took one look at the tattoo and then met my eye. "You tried to wash it off, didn't you?" he asked.

I nodded and felt my face turn red.

A few days later I started the process of laser removal. No matter which way I looked at it, it was better to pretend to be the person others wanted me to be than the person I longed to be.

"The worst crime is faking it."

—KURT COBAIN

YOUTUBE'S BIGGEST

I put my heart and soul into my channel and go from 100,000 subscribers to 6 million in just twelve months.

Before I moved to LA, my then-manager Mohammed told me I would get plenty of work just by living in the city, but after several months I still hadn't heard a word from him. It was a real kick in the teeth, and it meant I spent most of my time alone in my apartment. In the end, I couldn't bear any more of it, so I called my good friend Qias Omar from the Bay Area and asked if he wanted to move in with me.

Qias really was a source of inspiration to me, and luckily, he said yes. Or, more accurately, "Sure, I don't have anything better to do."

My apartment had a small walk-in closet, and just enough space for Qias to put in an inflatable mattress and a small desk for his computer.

In many ways Qias was my complete opposite; he was full of energy and seemed completely uninterested in any of the things that made my life a mess. Take the girl I was in a long-distance relationship with at the time.... We were always fighting over the phone, and when we weren't doing that, I was either getting drunk, smoking weed to numb my anxiety, or sneaking out of the house telling him I was running errands when I was really headed to a massage parlor. After watching me for a few days, Qias turned to me and said: "You're really messing up, man. You need to focus on your videos."

It was morning, and I was slumped on the couch with my THC pen in my mouth like usual, staring blankly ahead.

"You're wasting your time with her," he continued. "You should focus on your career. You should be grinding."

As hard as it was to hear what he was saying, I couldn't help but agree with him. Still, I found it hard to break my bad habits—or I did until I saw the film *Thanks for Sharing*, which is about three men undergoing a twelve-step program to recover from sexual addiction. I remember being glued to the screen, slack jawed and heart racing because I really recognized myself in one of the characters.

Not long later, I called my long-distance girlfriend to unburden my heart. She barely had time to answer before I blurted out: "Babe, there's something I need to tell you. I've got a sex addiction."

She was shocked, of course, and managed to say, "What are you talking about?"

Filled with my own instinct and a need to share my thoughts with someone, I didn't realize just how my words sounded. It didn't help that I awkwardly explained that my addiction revolved around happy endings at various massage parlors, porn, and excessive masturbation. She was silent for a moment, but then she started crying. It wasn't until long after we ended our increasingly awkward call that I realized just how much I'd hurt her. I called her again the next day to explain that it had nothing to do with her, but that made no difference. She sounded like I'd ruined her life and broke up with me before we even hung up. It wasn't until my first day in rehab receiving the white book that I read something along the lines of, "When you find out you have an addiction, you may feel very excited and a sudden urge to tell close ones around you about your addiction. DON'T. It is not right to share with them what you are going through until you are on your way to recovery." Oops.

Later that day, my manager called out of the blue.

"I have an audition in the works."

As I mentioned earlier, I hadn't heard from him since before I moved to LA, and I was still really bummed out from the call with my girlfriend, so my reply was pretty unenthusiastic: "OK...."

My manager didn't seem to care and waited for me to go on.

"What's the film?" I asked.

"*Fast and Furious 7.*"

His words lit some kind of hope in me, and I went to the audition for the part of "The Arab" the very next week.

I guess I did a good job because they said they were interested, and I remember calling my manager every single day afterward to see whether he had heard anything.

"The producer and I are meeting on Thursday," he told me, but when Thursday came around I didn't hear a peep out of him. When I called him up he was all evasive, and before long I realized that the part would never be mine—the producer had told him that I looked too young.

I remember I took it pretty hard, but my working life soon took a different turn—partly because Qias had moved in and partly because my manager called with a new approach.

"I found a camera guy who can help with your filming," he told me. He continued enthusiastically, "It's $500 per video, but you'll be able to produce, direct, and edit everything yourself."

The camera guy, Ali Baluch, and I clicked the minute we met, and we decided to make my first skit in LA. We filmed the first one and it took me all night to edit the material, and the next morning I posted it on YouTube. But almost at once, the video started to get loads of negative feedback. People didn't think it was as funny as my earlier videos, and that I'd made a big mistake moving to LA. Some people even declared that my career was over. As I read those comments I could feel anxiety creeping up on me, because I had a feeling they were right.

The following day, I was at the gym and noticed the way all the guys were staring at a girl's butt in yoga pants—and how uncomfortable she seemed with it.

Ali and I drove to Venice Beach the next day, and I remember explaining my idea to him as we drove. The minute we parked up, Ali grabbed the camera and ran off to hide.

I changed into a T-shirt and a pair of yoga pants, opened the trunk and waited for a guy to walk by. It was only a few minutes before I spotted a dude walking my way, and I went up to him and offered him twenty dollars to take part in my video. I explained what I wanted him to do word for word even down to his reactions, then I bent down over the trunk, sticking my ass in the air.

The guy pretended he thought I was a girl and couldn't tear his eyes off me, and that's when I stood up and asked him why he was staring at my butt. The guy was so taken aback that he didn't know what to do, and he stuttered something like, "Are you calling me gay?"

"Nah," I told him. "But, like, you looked at my butt. Is it big or something?"

We repeated the same prank with several guys, who all got twenty dollars. Every one of them stared at me, and everyone pretended to be as confused and humiliated as the first.

I clipped the video together that same night and gave it the title "Yoga Pants Prank." The cover image for the video was a close up of my butt in yoga pants which to be honest, looked like a really nice butt. It went viral pretty much right when it was uploaded. If I remember correctly, 1 million views in about an hour. Reality had struck as quick as the video hit 1 million views. Why continue to spend hours writing, acting, and editing a sketch video that people would hate on when I could go outside, film a prank video in thirty minutes, and get a way bigger response than a sketch ever could?

From that moment on, my life had changed for good. A week later, when we returned to Venice Beach to film a new prank, people kept stopping me and saying, "Oh my God, you're Fousey! I saw your prank!"

Before long, more established pranksters from YouTube started getting in touch, inviting me into their circles. We started hanging out, and it wasn't long before I heard them talking about "fake pranks."

"Hold up," I said, feigning surprise. "You *fake* your pranks?"

"Yeah, dude, everyone does."

Deep in thought, I went to see Qias Omar and Ali Baluch that evening.

"Guys," I said to them. "EVERYONE FAKES THEIR PRANKS. Why should we feel bad about it? Either we play the game to change the game, or we let the game play us and be those broke mother effers talking about staying true." A line I had previously heard from J. Cole.

I'm not trying to defend the decision I made in that moment, but from then on, I started faking all my pranks.

That year I went from 100,000 subscribers to 6 million, and before long I couldn't even walk down the street without someone coming up and talking to me or asking for a selfie. But I never took advantage of it. I never partied or became a part of the Hollywood scene, possibly because I still felt so alone with all my worries and insecurities. On the one hand, I was filming these videos with millions of views, becoming a superstar, but on the other I was struggling with who I was and what I was meant to do in life. No matter how much I achieved, it would never feel like enough. I was missing too much in my personal life. I had too many holes that needed to be filled.

It was around this time that I also dropped out of acting classes. I was doing so well and making so much money that I actually forgot I wanted to be an actor. Instead, I became increasingly obsessed with what people were writing about me in the comment section.

I started every day by checking my Twitter feed to see what people were saying to me. If I didn't get a lot of responses to a tweet, I'd feel anxious and angry with myself. But if I got a lot of attention, I felt like I was doing something great and that I was a good person. I got my validation from people on social media, not from those around me in my actual life. Social media became my drug. It defined who I was as a person and dictated who I saw when I looked at myself in the mirror. If people loved me that day, I loved myself. If people hated me, I hated myself. The funniest thing about it is I was being judged and hated for a persona I was putting on. So why was I taking it so personally? For example, if in a prank I did something extremely obnoxious and douchey, I was acting, the person being pranked was acting, and it was fake. The person I was in my real life was vastly different from the fousey-TUBE persona I had created. So why did I care?

"For sure, even the worst blow job
is better than, say, sniffing the best rose...
watching the greatest sunset.
Hearing children laugh."

—CHUCK PALAHNIUK

"A dog is the only thing on earth that loves
you more than you love yourself."

—JOSH BILLINGS

A DOLLAR AND A DREAM

Salvation comes on four legs.

The following winter, Qias had moved back to our hometown, Fremont, and I moved to a much larger apartment at 5200 Wilshire Boulevard, but I still wasn't remotely happy. This apartment I believe was $3,750 a month—a significant increase from Barrington being $2,400. I was working so much and so hard that I lost my grip and suddenly I weighed 245 pounds.

It was around this time that a friend came over to visit with her dog one day—a little Yorkshire Terrier I'd never met before.

I'd had a dog as a child, but only for one day. Mama was terrified of dogs, to the extent that she ran over to the other side of the road whenever we saw one on the sidewalk. In Muslim culture, there's an idea that dogs are unclean too, so you can't have them in the house. That's why, when I was twelve, after begging for a dog—and being given one by a kind friend of the family—she refused to let it sleep in the house.

Baba and my brothers helped me build a kennel for it in the yard, and when I hurried outside to see it the next morning, the dog was overjoyed to see me. I barely even managed to unclip its leash before it jumped up on me, barking and wagging its tail. The problem was that Mama had managed to pass her fear of dogs on to me, meaning that I was terrified by it and tried to run away.

Mama saw the whole thing happen from the kitchen window, and as I raced inside, gasping for air, she folded her arms and said, "Yousef, this is no good. You're not ready for a dog. We'll have to give it back."

The thought of having a dog of my own had never even crossed my mind since then—not until I saw my friend's amazing Yorkshire Terrier.

I drove out to see a breeder an hour outside of LA the very next day and asked whether they had any of the same breed available.

"Sure, we've got a bunch of them," she said with a smile.

She told me to follow her and introduced me to several incredibly cute Yorkshire Terriers, but there was one dog in particular that caught my eye—a female called Katrina, if I remember correctly. I held her in my arms for a while and then asked, "Can I buy this one?"

"Sure," said the breeder. "We just need to fill in a few forms. Come through to the office with me. You can take her away today."

Unfortunately, I had only just sat down at the woman's desk when Katrina started making all kinds of weird noises, and next thing I knew, she'd thrown up in my lap.

"Oh dear," said the breeder, getting to her feet to grab something to clean up the vomit. "She hasn't shown any sign of being ill. It's probably just something she ate."

Inexperienced as I was, I felt worried.

"Maybe she should stay here overnight," I said. "Then I'll come back tomorrow, once she's better, and take her home."

The breeder gave me a slightly strange look, but she agreed to it.

She met me at the door the next day when I went back to pick up Katrina.

"Hey, listen," she said. "I didn't realize you were a social media star. We've got a very unique Yorkie here. He's very small, very cute, and we were saving him for someone who could give our business some great exposure. I'd like you to meet him."

She went to fetch the dog, which turned out to be a little male who was full of character. I picked him up and he immediately started licking my face. I knew right away that he was the dog for me, and I also knew exactly what I'd call him: Dollar, after J. Cole's slogan, "A Dollar and a Dream."

Dollar quickly became my best friend. He came everywhere with me and was so small that I could carry him in my rucksack. His small size meant he had a hard time playing with bigger dogs, and that's probably one of the reasons I decided to go back to see the breeder and ask whether I could get a brother or sister for him not long later.

Around that time some of my YouTube friends had taken part in a program called "Insanity" where they were paid to work out and eat healthy food to lose weight for sixty days. Once the sixty days was up, I called the company and asked if I could join their next program. I was asked to audition which I did. I was brutally honest in the audition and vlogged the entire before and after. I explained how I hated who I had become. Hated what I saw when I looked in the mirror. And wanted to become a better version of myself. A couple of days later they called me and told me that I had been accepted but there was a catch. They told me they didn't have an influencer section anymore and therefore couldn't pay me for my participation. I said I could it do it without payment. Me changing my life was far greater than any monetary value.

The project was going to run for ninety days, under the name "Body Beast", and every morning I had to be at the gym on the dot of 9:00 AM. If I arrived late more than twice, I would be thrown out. After each training session I was given a bag of food, and when I got home I had to eat whatever was inside it, no more, no less.

I documented the whole thing, posted daily videos on my vlog YouTube channel called DOSEofFOUSEY and called it "The 90 Day Journey."

When I was done I had managed to drop to 179 pounds and was in the best—and thinnest—shape of my life. I posted a motivational video documenting the entire weight loss journey that people still come up and talk to me about till this day. I believe that video left the biggest impression on my audience. I mean in the beginning of the video I'm overweight talking about how unhappy I was and saying I was going to change my life in ninety days. By the end of the video a much younger, better looking, happier version of myself pops up on the screen giving validation to everything I had said. The crazy thing is, Body Beast is owned by the same company that I did the P90X infomercial for. Life had come full circle. This time I was not only in their infomercial, but the highlight of success. Again, using the law of attraction without noticing.

When it was time to get a new puppy, I had only just arrived when I saw a tiny little ball of white fluff running around. The dog wasn't a Yorkie. She was a Maltese, and she immediately started playing with Dollar. Terrorizing him actually. A short time later, I officially had a second dog, and I gave her the name Muffin.

If I'm perfectly honest—which is the point in a book like this—I don't know how I would have coped without my two dogs that spring. They woke me up every morning, jumping on me and licking my face, and no matter how bad I felt, I knew they depended on me to take care of them and give them food. It was the first time I was able to find responsibility and purpose outside of myself.

"I'm just enjoying my life.
I suggest you try it."

—TYLER PERRY

MY ACTING CAREER

People become convinced that I'm faking depression in order to gain new viewers, and Tyler Perry asks me to be in his film.

L ate that summer, I was sitting in the car with Ali Baluch when I got a message saying I was nominated for Show of the Year at the fifth annual Streamy Awards. I was overjoyed, because the other nominees were the biggest stars on YouTube. By this point I had long had a deep faith in the "Law of Attraction," thanks to a book that's very near and dear to my heart called *The Secret* by Rhonda Byrne. So a few days later, when I was driving with Ali on Highway 1, I took out my vlog camera and told my vlog audience "The BRUH BRUHS" who watched me on DOSEofFOUSEY which had amassed 4 million subscribers, that they needed to vote for me if I was going to win: "Guys, you know I believe in law of attraction...how cool would it be if the Streamys airs on VH1, and they say: 'And the winner is...fouseyTUBE,' and I walk on stage and as I accept my award I say: 'I'd like to dedicate this award to all of my DOF BRUH BRUHS.'"

A couple of months later, I went to the gala with Ali and my new assistant, and I'll never forget how I felt when they called out my name as the winner and I went up on stage and said what I had said I would say. In that moment, it was like all my problems had disappeared. I had proven to my entire audience that you can speak what you want in life into existence. That same week I was invited into a meeting with one of LA's most famous agencies. I was making so much noise in the social media scene that they wanted to sign me and take full control of my career. This was just the beginning.

Unfortunately, the feeling of joy didn't last long. By weeks end the award had lost all meaning. *Everything* had lost all meaning, and over the weeks that followed, I spent most of my time on the couch at home, staring out at the terrace on the other side of the panoramic windows, fantasizing about climbing up onto the railing and swinging my legs over the edge for a moment before slamming down onto the asphalt below. It was bizarre. I was making more money than I could ever have imagined. Was one of the most viewed channels on YouTube. Had just been signed to one of LA's biggest agencies. Yet still found myself depressed and unhappy with myself.

It wasn't the thoughts or the images that scared me but the fact that they felt more appealing than *anything*. One afternoon, as I was sitting at my laptop like usual, I felt so down that I turned on the webcam and started talking openly to my fans—not just about my depression but about my addiction and how impossible it felt to break free. I had never told them what my addiction was out of embarrassment and for the sake of keeping at least one thing private in my personal life. Since I was daily vlogging there was very little I held back from telling my audience. I told them how I was feeling every single day throughout every single moment. And you can imagine, being bipolar that means in the first part of the vlog I could be extremely happy as if I was about to conquer the world. But by the end I could be crying saying that I had lost another battle to my addiction and had fallen into a deep depression.

Sadly, it didn't take long before the comments box filled up with people questioning how truthful I was being. A lot of people were convinced I was faking depression in order to gain new viewers, and others were sure I was joking. "He's lying about having an addiction. He's just keeping us guessing for views." If only they knew how real it was.

I had been lying awake in bed for hours one day, unable to get up, when the phone started ringing. If I hadn't seen my new agent's name on the screen, I probably wouldn't have picked up, but I reluctantly hit accept and heard my agent's enthusiastic voice: "Hey Yousef...we thought it was just a prank call, but it seems like Tyler Perry wants to speak with you."

"Tyler Perry?" I thought it sounded like a joke myself.

"Here, let me give you his number so you can get in touch with him."

When we ended the call, I sat up on the edge of the bed and rubbed my head repeatedly. Why did Tyler want to talk to me? The only way to find out was to call the number my agent had just messaged over.

I decided to use FaceTime purely to make sure it really wasn't all a bad joke. As it happened, it wasn't. After just a few rings, Tyler's face appeared on the screen, and I barely had time to say hello before he said, "Hey, man. I saw your videos. They made me laugh when I was feeling really down."

I liked him right away. There was something about the seriousness and the honesty in his voice that appealed to me, and instead of sucking up to him and just telling him how much I enjoyed his films growing up, I decided to open up about my depression, my insecurities, and the demons I was constantly battling. Tyler listened patiently and then told me about some of the difficult periods he'd gone through himself.

He called me again a few weeks later. "Yo, I'm working on a movie called *Boo! A Madea Halloween*, and I want you in it. Just let me know what character you want to play."

After my breakthrough on YouTube, I'd put all dreams of becoming an actor on ice, so being offered a role in a Tyler Perry film was more than I ever could have dreamed of. Even crazier, a few years earlier in an interview I had dubbed myself as "the Middle Eastern Tyler Perry" since he is where I got my inspiration from during my phase of making Middle Eastern content. Maybe that's why I immediately blurted out, "I want a lead role," without even pausing to think.

Everything happened super quickly after that. Tyler gave me the role of the president of a fraternity and sent over a script for me to read. I told him I'd get more social media influencers on board and gave him the names of a few people I thought would be a great fit—people who would be able to bring a huge amount of attention to the film.

Tyler took me at my word, and in mid-January 2016, filming got underway in Atlanta. It was my first ever movie shoot, so everything felt both exciting and daunting, but above all it was just so new.

For one thing, I had to go from makeup to costume early in the morning, followed by a whole bunch of other areas, and when the time to shoot finally came 'round several hours later, Tyler called over everyone from the first scene for a pep talk.

I was the lead actor in the very first scene and suddenly found myself standing there with every camera on me. I felt my heart rate increase and then Tyler shouted, "Action!"

I said my line like I was in some kind of trance and heard Tyler say, "OK, great! Do it one more time."

He shouted action and I delivered my line again, still feeling like someone else was saying them.

"OK, great!" said Tyler, looking away. "Moving on."

"Wait, wait!" I shouted. "That was just me rehearsing. What do you mean by moving on? I didn't get it. I didn't do it."

Tyler turned back to me and smiled. "What are you talking about? You were perfect."

With that, he walked off to film the next scene.

I was left behind, wondering if this was how a movie shoot worked. Was everything at this pace? I soon found out that it was—at least when Tyler was directing—and I realized that what I delivered on the first or second take was what would end up in the movie. It meant I had to perform at my very best the whole time, in every take and in every scene.

Despite that, I loved every second of it and never wanted it to end. Most of that is down to Tyler himself for creating such a great mood among the actors and letting my sister come along to set one day.

When she was young, my sister had dreamed of being an actress, but Mama and Baba didn't let her because she was a girl and it wasn't a good look in our culture. So when she came to the set, it felt good to be able to tell her that Tyler had said she could be an extra if she wanted. When it was almost time for her to go back to the airport, I asked one of the other actors—a YouTuber, just like me—if he knew where Tyler was. Because Noura wanted the opportunity to thank him.

"Yeah, I just saw him over there," he said, pointing to the costume department.

Noura and I walked over and immediately spotted him standing with his back to us. He had gotten into costume as his character, Madea—meaning he was made up like an old woman, with a blonde wig, granny glasses, and a floral dress.

"Hey Tyler," I said. "This is my sister, she wanted to say hi."

Tyler wheeled around and stared at us with a look of horror on his face.

"Are you crazy? Why are you introducing me to your sister when I look like this?" With both hands, he gestured to his old lady outfit. It was obvious that he was joking so I decided to play along.

"Oh, I'm sorry," I said, holding my hands up and pretending to be crushed and deeply remorseful.

But Tyler just laughed and said hello to Noura, who was grinning like mad. She seemed delighted to see that my childhood dream had come true.

"It was funny, too, how lonesome a person could be in a crowded house."

—CARSON MCCULLERS

UNIVERSALLY ADORED

I make my family proud
for the very first time.

I had only just got back from Atlanta when I signed the lease on the biggest penthouse in a new apartment complex at 1600 Vine Street in Hollywood. I was twenty-six at the time on my sixth year of YouTube and this was before it was cool to show off your "YouTube Money" and buy extravagant houses. Till this day, this is one of my biggest financial regrets that would alter my life forever. It cost me $13,500 a month and quickly became the world's most expensive isolation cell. There were a bunch of other social media stars living right next door—people like Logan and Jake Paul and Lele Pons—who weren't on YouTube at that time, but on an app called Vine. I never knocked on their doors, and I never invited them over to my place. The only friends I hung out with were Alex Wassabi and his brother Aaron. They lived right next door to my unit and I would go into their place as a safe haven whenever I felt the courage to step out of my cell.

Maybe it's because friendship has always been a really difficult thing for me. I was still working with Ali, but the truth is that I didn't have any close friends who were really there for me, people I could share my deepest thoughts and feelings with. I know that other people are great at making friends, but I've never known how to strike up that connection with another person, and I've also noticed that other people don't know how to get through to me. I always felt like people didn't like me much. Probably because I didn't like myself. Or at least who I really was.

The entire situation was as tragic as it was absurd. I mean, I was making a whole bunch of money and living in a dream world where everything was handed to me on a plate, where everything was accessible. I had an endless amount of girls after me, I could just pull out a credit card and buy anything I needed, life was limitless. All I had to do was come up with two YouTube videos a month. I guess maybe that was the problem. Since I could sleep in as late as I wanted, I often didn't get up until three or four o'clock in the afternoon. I would drink coffee while I thought about what to post on social media, and once I came up with an idea, I posted the result. After that, I would do a long session at the gym before slumping down in front of my computer to watch a movie and eat junk food, eventually managing to fall asleep at some point in the early hours. Either that or I'd drive over to one of the massage parlors nearby, paying the masseuse extra for a happy ending to take my mind off things and ease my anxiety. The thing is, none of that seemed to work. In fact, it became a compulsive behavior that soon took up way too much of my weird existence where I just drifted around on my own.

It's actually kind of amazing that I managed to produce so many videos and accomplish so much success. My fans really must have seen me as someone with a never-ending supply of energy, someone who came up with all kinds of crazy ideas and gave motivational speeches in between. Whenever the red light for the camera was on, I was a different animal. No matter how depressed I was or what I was going through, I would light up an entire room with my persona. But in reality, I was a completely different person: deeply insecure, lonely, convinced no one would ever love me, and trapped in a worsening sex addiction that, because of my Muslim upbringing, filled me with an unbearable sense of shame.

At the same time, I went from being the black sheep of the family to the star. My face started appearing on billboards all over the place, and in October 2016, when the premiere of *Boo! A Madea Halloween* came 'round, I got to do something I'd had on my bucket list for as long as I could remember: walk my mama and baba across a Hollywood red carpet.

Mama looked amazing, which made me happy and proud. It felt great that I had the opportunity to create this special moment for her. Baba was also dressed up, and the pictures of the three of us outside the movie theater were published in a bunch of papers and online. They became proof somehow that I'd achieved my dreams. It was the new biggest moment of my life, and it felt like, from there, the only way was up. When the movie released, it had become number one in the box office for three to four weeks.

"People don't need love. What they need is success in one form or another."

—CHARLES BUKOWSKI

ENTERTAINER OF THE YEAR

I misspeak and spark a hate storm.

A round the same time that *Boo! A Madea Halloween* had its premiere, I was nominated for Entertainer of the Year at the next year's Streamy Awards, and this time I took the girl I was dating to the gala at the Beverly Hilton. With her by my side on the red carpet in her figure-hugging red dress, paparazzi flashes blazing, the whole thing felt a little like a dream. That feeling hung around all evening and was still there as we sat at our table waiting for the winners to be announced. What's crazy is, I knew that I would be announced as the winner. I had used the law of attraction and spoken it into existence for months prior. I remember having a chat with my agent at CAA and telling her, "Be sure to get a good pic of me while I'm accepting my award on stage."

From a purely professional point of view, the past year had gone exceptionally well, though I was probably also the YouTuber with the most drama at the time. The channel Drama Alert had recently exposed my fake pranks, for example, and since I didn't have a team around me (and was also struggling with my bipolar disorder), I dealt with that by announcing that *everyone* did fake pranks. The only problem was that none of the other influencers were willing to admit that was true, which meant a whole bunch of people thought I was the only one; they decided that I'd cheated my way to success. This was my downfall. Never knowing how to handle the hate. It wasn't until years later when Logan Paul and Jake Paul had become the stars that I once was that I saw that everyone at the top gets hate. But the key was to ignore it. If only I had known.

Still, despite all that, it felt like my true followers had finally gained an insight into the real Yousef, and they seemed to like what they saw. I was very open and honest with my bouts of depression. No matter how good my life was going, I wasn't scared to post a video crying in shame saying that I was depressed and unhappy. I guess most people recognized themselves in me and saw no point judging or casting suspicion on me. I was open about being depressed and suffering from bipolar but still showing everyone that nothing could hold me back if I put my mind to it. At the same time, I knew—as I sat there with my girlfriend, talking to friends and colleagues who came over to say hi—that there were still people out there who wanted me to fail, and that occasionally made me zone out so completely that she took my hand and, with a concerned look on her face, said, "Are you OK, babe? Are you nervous?"

"Nah," I said, shaking my head. "I was just thinking about what to say when I win."

She laughed and gave me a tender glance.

It was neither the time nor the place to tell her how I really felt. Would she even be able to understand me if I explained how much it bothered me that so many strangers wanted to see me suffer? I could just hear what she would say: "But that's just because you've reached the top, babe. Everyone successful has a load of haters."

The problem was that my bipolar disorder meant I was badly equipped to deal with it. It made no difference how hard I tried not to let it get to me when people called me fake, ugly, weak, lame, or told me to kill myself and die, it just kept swirling around in my head, even after the awards ceremony got underway. When the host for the evening, called out my name as winner of Entertainer of the Year, I felt an almost overwhelming sense of triumph.

Maybe that was why I completely forgot what I had been planning to say as I stepped onto the stage. I had no choice but to improvise and heard myself saying something along the lines of, "This year I became one of the most hated YouTubers on the platform. I achieved this despite all the shit I got." I repeated some of the names I'd been called over the past year, but as I said "gay" I noticed that the room went silent.

It was only afterward, when I read all the comments online, that I realized how people had taken the things I said. I guess it was my defiant tone that made it sound like I thought being gay was a bad thing, which wasn't my intention at all. Just like that, I found myself being labelled as a homophobe, and people even started making videos about it. I also got accused of cheating my way to the award, by organizing competitions on my channel so that my followers would vote for me. If I was a stronger person, I probably would've just shrugged and laughed it off, then moved on with my life by focusing on all the positives—like my girlfriend, my success, or the award I won the night before.

But just as it had at the start of my career, every negative judgement cut straight through me. The only difference was that there were so many more than ever before because I had so many more followers. It was no longer a wave of hate; it was a tsunami, and I was completely incapable of dealing with it.

"When you're on the road, you don't really have to deal with real life. It's almost like hitting the pause button."

—TAYLOR JENKINS REID

TOURS

Roman Atwood and I enjoy success in the States, Canada, and England.

There are some people who are constantly searching for their next audience. Without it, they don't exist, or worse: they're all alone. I guess I must be one of them, because ever since my first gig, which I did while I was still living at home with Mama and Baba, I had been longing to get back on the stage.

Back when I did that first gig, I had just started my YouTube channel and appeared on a livestream on a site called U-Stream, where I said, "I wish I could be in a position where I could talk to you guys on stage and tell you my story and help motivate you."

The very next day, I got a message from a stranger. He wrote: "Hey, saw you on U-Stream yesterday. A few of us here in Ocala, Florida, are planning an event, and we'd like you to come down here and take part."

I remember feeling so overwhelmed that I said yes right away, and soon received a plane ticket.

A week or so later, one of the organizers came to meet me at the Ocala Airport. The guy was around the same age as me, and he drove me to my hotel. After he'd helped me check in, he said, "You have to come over to my place to eat and meet my family."

"Uh, sure," I said, not really understanding what he meant.

An hour later, he came back to pick me up, and the minute we arrived at his place, I realized his family prepared a whole dinner for me. They met me in the hallway along with his siblings and a couple cousins, plus the friends he was organizing the event with.

It felt intimate to say the least, and maybe that's why it didn't occur to me to turn to the guy who picked me up until after we ate and ask, "Is there anything in particular you want me to talk about tonight?"

I assumed they might have a particular angle they wanted me to take in the motivational speech I'd been preparing over the past week.

But the guy smiled at me over the table.

"Nah, just do your thing like usual," he said.

"My thing?"

"Yeah, you know, your comedy act."

His words took me completely by surprise, but I managed to keep my cool. As soon as I got back to my room at the hotel, I sat down and started writing a few bullet points on a piece of paper before he came back to get me to take me to the event. I locked myself in the bathroom when we arrived, and threw up from nerves.

Before long, it was my turn to take to the stage, and I remember looking out at the audience as though I was in a daze. I could see from their faces that they expected to laugh non-stop for the next thirty never-ending minutes.

I swallowed, glanced at my phone, and told my first joke. I think it was about Mama, but I'm not completely sure; I entered a state of mind where I barely knew what I was saying or doing. But to my huge relief and surprise, it worked. The audience was laughing harder and harder, particularly when I did impressions of Mama, Baba, my grandma, and aunt. When I left the stage, people were thumping me on the back and congratulating me, and I experienced it all with the strange sense of miraculously having survived a car crash without a single scratch.

It didn't take long for another feeling to take over: gratitude at having been able to take part, plus a powerful longing to do it again. I had done many stand up tours the years that followed and always made sure to end my show with a motivational speech. Still having a burning desire to be a motivational speaker.

Remembering all this in 2016, I told my agent at CAA that I'd love to do a few shows. I continued: "I know this sounds crazy, but I'm really good friends with Roman Atwood, and I think that if I asked him to go on tour with me, he would say yes."

Roman and I were two of the biggest YouTube stars at the time, and when I couldn't handle the loneliness in my apartment, I used to go home with Roman to his family in Ohio, where we would do crazy things every day. One time I flipped Romans ATV buggy while trying to do donuts, and another time we had a firework war with roman candles, and we went to a shooting range and fired at explosives. Roman always wanted to live life to the fullest, and would often tell me that I had to smile even though life didn't give me any reason to. He always stood by me, no matter what people said or wrote about me online.

Anyway, as soon as I left the meeting with my agent, I called him. Roman thought the idea was so great that we soon put together a ninety-minute show. The first half was a comedy act, the second more motivational. We rehearsed for a few weeks and then set out on the road across much of the United States and parts of Canada.

I was pretty used to fans coming up and wanting to talk and take selfies with me, but I was completely blown away by the reception we got in the cities we visited. There were huge crowds waiting for us no matter where we went, and every show was sold out. That was pretty much down to Roman, because he was a real superstar. My role was to be the one the audience booed when we were introduced and played out our pretend beef on stage.

We quickly found our feet in terms of the show too. As ever, I did quite a lot of solo improvisation, but we also did skits and challenges together, like when we invited someone up onto the stage at the end of the show and said, "Is it cool if we shave your hair off?" We also came up with our own backstage prep as we listened to the people outside chanting "ROMAN! ROMAN! ROMAN! FOUSEY! FOUSEY! FOUSEY!"

We were met by the cheers of thousands of people every time we came out on stage, and it gave us such a kick that we delivered epic performances night after night.

There was always a whole load of fans waiting for us by our tour bus every night, and they would tell me just how much of an impact I'd had on their lives. Both Roman and I felt like rock stars, though we never behaved like them. Our tight tour schedule, combined with the fact that Roman had young kids and a girlfriend he loved (and that I'd just met my girlfriend), meant we barely partied at all. The hysteria around us meant we preferred to stay on the tour bus, talking to each other. It was like we needed to vent about the crazy experience we were both going through so we could laugh about it. We always reminded each other after each show that we were living through a once-in-a-lifetime experience, and to never take advantage of the situation we were in.

Since the tour was such a success, we were constantly adding new dates, and it didn't take long before we were booked outside of North America. I took my girlfriend to a few gigs, among them in London. There was talk about taking a trip to the Middle East, but Roman decided he couldn't handle being away from his family any longer, so we broke the whole thing off.

More than anything, what I got from the tour life was what I gained from being around Roman. He was a role model, mentor, and an older brother to me all at the same time. He taught me so much about life and was like a light in the darkness during my hard times. One thing I'll never forget was what he taught me about relationships. Normally on YouTube, a couple is all lovey-dovey and portrayed as goals on camera, but off camera you couldn't even tell they were together. There was a business type relationship instilled in their bond. But with Roman, one thing I'll never forget is it wasn't when the camera was on that he was the perfect boyfriend to his (now wife)—but when the cameras were off. One time in specific, he recorded a whole bit with his girlfriend Brittney and it wasn't until he stopped recording that he grabbed her hand and pulled her in tight. Till this day, I am forever grateful for meeting Roman Atwood.

**"Love your haters—
they're your biggest fans."**

—KANYE WEST

REHAB

I get $120,000 to shake Kanye West's hand and realize I need help.

Coming home after months on the road was a brutal change. I was still high on the validation I got every night on stage and so full of energy that I just had to do something with it. Maybe that was why, a few weeks after I got back to Los Angeles, Mama and Baba invited me to go to Istanbul.

I had dreamed of going to the ancient city for years and of visiting all the incredible sights like the Blue Mosque and the Hagia Sophia. I was curious to see how East meets West there, and saw the vacation as the perfect mix of relaxation and education.

The plan was to spend two weeks in Istanbul, but we had barely even landed when I got a call from my agent.

"Hey, so...Verizon is having this event.... Kanye West is going to perform, and all you have to do is attend. They're offering a fee of $120,000."

"Uh...OK," I said. "So all I have to do is walk the red carpet before a private Kanye West concert?"

"Exactly!" my agent confirmed, adding, "You might also have to greet him on stage."

There wasn't much to think about, so I explained the situation to my parents and made sure they would enjoy the rest of their time in Istanbul before I got on the next plane back to LA.

Not once during the flight did I think about how fortunate I was to be earning so much money for going to a concert with the biggest artist on earth—and getting to greet him too. The truth is that I was so spoiled with work and collaborations at the time that it almost felt normal. I truly believed that the lifestyle I was living would be forever.

But 2016–2017 weren't simply the years I made my Hollywood debut, won the biggest awards at the Streamys as Entertainer of the Year for the second year in a row, went on a successful tour, and earned millions. It was also the year I realized I had no choice but to seek help for my sex addiction.

My sexuality had been fundamentally messed up since I was a kid, but over time it had become my way of repressing my feelings. Above all, I used masturbation and massage parlors to numb the panicked anxiety that occasionally took over my life.

When our world tour ended and I suddenly found myself with so much free time on my hands, my addiction worsened. Masturbation and visiting massage parlors for happy endings were no longer my little escape from the world; they began to make me feel increasingly ashamed and unhappy.

A few weeks after I got home, I checked into rehab for the second time. The first time had been a couple of years before, when I was spending a lot of time with two of my best YouTube friends at the time. Back then, they used to have to drive me to an addiction clinic in LA three times a week. They didn't know what I was going to rehab for but respected my privacy. I sat in a circle with four other men and a supervisor, and we talked. One of the men talked about compulsively visiting strip clubs, another about buying sex from hundreds of prostitutes, and so on. We talked openly not just about our problems but our childhoods, too, though I soon felt that this wasn't going to help me deal with my problems. I just couldn't manage to engage with the group in the way the supervisor wanted me to. We were asked to call one another at least once per day. I never made a single call. Even when it would be

10:00 AM and my mind would convince me to drive to a massage parlor instead of an important meeting and every fiber in my body would tell me to call one of my rehab companions so they could help talk me out of it, I wouldn't. Maybe it was a defense mechanism, but it meant I dropped out of the program early and quickly got back into my old routine of addiction.

When I checked into rehab this time, I took it way more seriously. I followed the treatment program to the letter and noted down everything they said and did all the tasks they asked me to do. I also started to go to group meetings organized by the SAA in Los Angeles once a week. SAA stands for Sex Addicts Anonymous, and the people there helped me realize I was suffering from an addiction that would be with me for the rest of my life, and which I was therefore going to have to consciously and actively fight every day. I also realized how much my life had been affected by that time my mom caught me touching myself as a child. It was reassuring to learn that I had an "intimacy disorder" which helped me put a lot of my problems into perspective. Not being able to connect with others but dying to do so suddenly made complete sense.

One thing I never understood in rehab and still have trouble understanding today is why is what I do considered an addiction to me and brings nothing but shame and guilt into my life, but so many males that I know take pride in going to massage parlors, paying for prostitutes, and masturbating daily? What differentiates why I do it to why they do it? Why are they OK with what they do while it makes me hate myself? I still can't give myself an answer.

While I was attending those group meetings, I was cast in a YouTube Red movie, a YouTube Red show, a cameo in a Netflix movie, and starred in another Tyler Perry Movie, *Boo 2! A Madea Halloween*. The producer for the Netflix movie was so happy with my cameo that he wanted me to meet with him for the possibility of doing a full movie on my own.

Sadly, that coincided with another depressive phase I had fallen into, and I slept in the day we were supposed to meet. He never gave me a second chance.

Things got even worse when I tried to switch to another agent at CAA. I wasn't happy with my current one because I thought she'd messed up a meeting with DJ Khaled who I had dreamed of meeting for a long time. When I got to his house, it turned out that he had no idea who I was or why I was there—the whole thing was just embarrassing. I also knew that my agent was planning to leave CAA and start her own management company, which was forbidden. So when I approached another agent at CAA and he spoke to my current agent, she got scared that I was going to reveal what she was planning. She called me to a meeting in a coffee shop the next day. I wasn't sure what the meeting was about and barely had time to sit down and order before she fixed her eyes on me and said: "Yousef, I really just wanted to let you know that CAA will no longer be representing you."

I stared at her in shock. "What do you mean? Have I been kicked out of the agency?"

She got up, leaving the money for her coffee on the table.

"Yes," she said. "You're being let go. You don't add enough value to CAA for us to keep you."

I knew that was a lie, because of everything I had done and all the things I had going on. There was no doubt that I was one of their most profitable YouTubers, but before I had time to say anything she walked off and I was left behind, feeling numb. I eventually managed to get up, tears streaming down my cheeks as I stepped outside. I pulled out my phone and called Tyler Perry, telling him what had happened.

"I don't know what to do," I sobbed. "I don't know how to find another agency."

Till this day, whenever a manager of mine asks CAA if they'd like to represent me, they reply saying that they remember having a bad time representing me and that they have no interest.

"Follow your inner moonlight;
don't hide the madness."

—ALLEN GINSBERG

PROJECT BUTTERFLY

I lose my best friend.

A few days after I was dropped by my agent, I found out that my secret girlfriend at the time, who my audience knew nothing about, had been playing me for the longest time. The news came as a crushing blow. Sure, it was hardly the first time I'd broken up with a girl, but it was definitely the first time I'd experienced real heartbreak. I didn't know how to deal with it and ended up calling my friends, talking on the phone for hours about my feelings without really working out how to numb my anxiety.

When I wasn't using my phone as a lifeline, I was sitting in my apartment with zero desire to do anything. I was a crazy mess and reverted to not wanting to get out of bed on certain days. At the same time, I felt a huge amount of pressure to deliver content to my channels to remain relevant. That hunt for fame really did stress me out, and maybe that's why, in the spring of 2017 when my rental period for the apartment at 1600 Vine was coming to an end, I decided to grab the bull by the horns and relieve myself of all responsibility and commitments. It would also enable me to leave behind everything that reminded me of the love I had lost.

In practice, that meant shipping a bunch of stuff to my parents, putting the rest into storage, and closing all my bank accounts so I wouldn't have any access to my money. I dropped off Dollar and Muffin with a dog sitter and walked out of the apartment with nothing but a backpack and the kindness of others to rely on.

Daniela, my videographer at the time, came with me to film the whole thing—something I'd hurriedly decided to call Project Butterfly.

During the first few days, we wandered the streets, asking complete strangers if they could give us either something to eat or let us crash at their places.

People's reactions were mixed. Some wanted to help us and others just didn't want to listen to us. But when I texted my big YouTube friends, they all stepped right up. We spent the first night on Logan Paul's famous bus, for example, which was parked outside Chase Bank on La Brea Avenue. After that, we spent time crashing with RiceGum, Amanda Cerny, and FaZe Rug, among others.

What I hadn't taken into consideration was how hard it would be to produce a new video every day. The norm on YouTube back then was to upload new content on a daily basis. My followers and I also had pretty high expectations when it came to quality, and that wasn't exactly easy to maintain while we were bumming around like that. This was the main reason I was super grateful when I got an offer from a company that wanted to contribute to Project Butterfly by sending us to watch an NBA finals game between the Cleveland Cavaliers and my "home" team, the Golden State Warriors.

On July 4, Daniela and I flew to San Francisco and then travelled on to Oakland, the Warriors' hometown. Before we left, I'd decided to take someone who was a huge fan of both me and the Warriors to the game. Through my channels, I managed to find a super young kid living in a suburb of the Bay Area.

Sitting there in the front row, it ended up being an unforgettable experience for both him and I—especially because the Warriors won the game.

Before we left the arena, I said to Daniela, "You know what would be cool? Let's go visit my old high school before we leave; we can see if anyone is a fan of me there." I wanted a chance to show the students of my home town that they could make it in life and be anything they wanted to become.

Daniela thought it sounded like a great idea, so on the following Monday afternoon, we showed up unannounced at my high school. Doing so was illegal at the time—school rules say that in order to be on campus, you have to have permission—but I just walked through the doors like I owned the place. Daniela had brought her camera, and the students started going wild. Next thing I knew there was a mob of hundreds of them all around me, jumping, cheering, and going crazy.

I was totally overwhelmed and felt a little like a hometown hero. Either that or someone who meant a lot to a bunch of people, in any case.

Sadly, the school leadership wasn't anywhere near as happy with my unexpected visit, and the police soon showed up to drive us away.

That didn't matter to me because we had to hurry over to the airport to catch a plane to Qatar. Some friends of Daniela had invited us over, wanting to contribute to Project Butterfly. They had paid for our tickets, and after a fifteen-hour flight, we landed in Doha with absolutely no idea what we would be doing there.

Daniela's friend, Kimo Basha, came to meet us at the airport, and I went out with him in town later that night. It turned out that the Doha nightlife scene was pretty quiet—at least it was until this big, bearded dude in traditional clothing came up to us, upset because we were filming. He demanded to see our visas and passports. I tried to explain that we had just arrived from San Francisco and that it hadn't been my intention to upset him, but the man kept getting increasingly angry and physical. I was obviously shocked but not as shocked as I was when the dude suddenly fell into Daniela's friend's arms, crying with laughter.

The whole thing was a prank, and for once, I was on the receiving end of it.

No matter how overwhelming it was to be in the Middle East or how funny and welcoming all the people there turned out to be, I got increasingly stressed out at having to film and edit new videos every day. Project Butterfly should have been a weekly project with one video on Sunday recapping all we had done. Not a daily look into the adventure. It was unrealistic and damn near impossible considering the Wi-Fi connections we had being abroad. I also got sick, and when the news reached me that there was something wrong with Dollar, I caught the next plane back to LA.

I took Dollar to see a vet, who said that the best thing would be to keep him under observation for a few days. He still wasn't well when I picked him up, so I decided to fly out to the east coast with him, Muffin, Kimo, and Daniela so we could stay with my parents for a while in Princeton, New Jersey. Earlier that year I had purchased a home for my parents there. It was directly across from my brother Mohammed's house and I thought it could be a cool little getaway for me when LA became too much and it would give my parents a chance to be near their grandkids.

I had only been there a few days when I heard Baba shouting at the top of his voice as I came out of the shower.

"Yousef, Yousef, come down here!"

I wrapped a towel around my waist and hurried downstairs. Dollar was lying on the floor in the living room, having a terrible seizure.

"No, no, no!" I shouted. I quickly got dressed and jumped into the car with Dollar, tears streaming down my cheeks. I drove to a nearby vet, and after storming into the examination room with my beloved four-legged friend in my arms, the vet examined him.

"I'm so sorry," the vet told me an hour or so later when he came out into the waiting room to talk to me. "If we decide to try to keep Dollar alive, it will be a life of pain. In my eyes, it would be better to put him down."

Dollar was only three, so I just couldn't understand how that could be the best option. It made zero sense to me. He was my first dog—my best friend—and I wasn't ready to lose him. At the same time, I obviously didn't want to see him suffer. I took him back to my parents' house so that they and my brothers could say goodbye, and I let him play on the lawn in the back yard one last time. After that, I drove him back to the vet and held him in my arms as the veterinarian euthanized him.

Two days later, I received a box containing his remains. Baba had prepared a burial site in the backyard, and we buried him later that day, creating a beautiful shrine and memorial for him there.

"You started rapping when you wasn't good at basketball. I started rapping because I needed Adderall."

—DONALD GLOVER

HATE DIES, LOVE ARRIVES

*I go into a manic phase
and decide to save the world.*

The next few days were difficult to process. And on one sunny day while I was lying in my brother Mohammed's pool looking over at my parents' house, which I had bought for them on the other side of the street, it occurred to me that instead of going back to Los Angeles and involving myself in all the chaos there, I could actually live with them. Because it was a big house and I could have the basement to myself.

So I moved across the street right away. And now a super strange thing happened. Mama had never liked dogs, but she suddenly started to feel sorry for Muffin, fussing over her because she had lost her best friend Dollar. I saw it with my own eyes one day when I came into the kitchen just as Mama picked up Muffin from the floor and sat down with her on her lap on the couch.

Mama soon started feeding Muffin every day—she even took her on walks—and before we knew it, the dog had become her new best friend.

For my part, I decided to renovate the basement, turning it into the ultimate bachelor pad. I could go down there and play my music as loud as I liked, but whenever I wanted my family's love, all I had to do was head back upstairs.

I also started a new channel called The Kats Family, after fouseyTUBE had reached 10 million subscribers and my vlog channel DOSEofFOUSEY hit 4 million subscribers. The Kats Family was a channel built around following the lives of the Erakats. I also launched a stream on Twitch. Twitch is a platform where you can chat with an audience live, play video games, or just hang out. The audience has the ability to give you donations and buy sub badges to show support. It was a good source of income. Late one evening, I heard myself say: "I wish I had some weed right now, but I don't know how to get it in New Jersey."

Five minutes later I got a text from a random number: "I'm a fan and I can supply you with weed."

I immediately texted back, "Here's my address. Come over!"

Not long later, the guy was standing outside.

Without even thinking about it, I welcomed him in. We went straight down to the basement and jumped on stream. I started smoking. It didn't take me long to realize that Ahmed aka Abreezy was an incredibly funny guy. He made me laugh more than anyone had in years, and he also lived just five minutes away. I invited him over again the next evening, and we did another Twitch stream together.

Over the next few months, we streamed together and I got high every single night without my parents knowing, and I felt happier than I had in a long while. So happy that I bought my first supercar—a Ferrari 488. Baba came with me when I went to buy it, and it really was a huge moment for me. I was able to do so because of the money I was saving from no longer having to pay insanely expensive rent living in LA. Still, just a few months later I decided I needed an even better car, so I swapped the Ferrari for a Spyder version (convertible) of the 488 and eventually bought myself a Range Rover Sport SVR.

One day around this time, I posted a video in which I said, "Guys, I'm in a very happy place right now. Things are going really good, so I'm going to try to live life without relying on medication."

The real reason I was ready to ditch my medications and had been so happy was that a friend had recently introduced me to Adderall, which gave me access to feelings I had never experienced before and allowed me to believe in myself again. It made me feel creative and gave me so much energy that I could film and upload a YouTube video, stay up all night on Twitch, get a few hours' sleep, wake up, take another Adderall, and be on it again. To be blunt, Adderall made me think I'd found the best version of myself, and whenever I struggled to get more from friends and acquaintances, I got my psychiatrist to prescribe it for me instead. Adderall made me feel like I believed I should have felt like my whole life. Free of depression and self-doubt and hate.

The problem was that I couldn't see that I was heading toward a manic phase in my bipolar disorder, and that, combined with the amphetamine-like medication, was only ever going to end in tears.

My thoughts became extremely big (manic), and I started to have the most grandiose ideas about what I wanted to do with my life and my future. I started announcing that I was going to write a book, make $3 million in a couple of months, and take my life to the next level by being a motivational speaker. To be honest, everything was driven out of wanting to feed my ego. Living in New Jersey and starting a new channel, I no longer had the fame I once had while living in LA and I wanted to feel it again. I wanted to show everyone who I was and what I was capable of and leave no doubts to my supporters that I was still able to reign on top of the YouTube scene. My reputation hadn't been what it once was because of all the various bouts of depression I had fallen into that caused me to leave YouTube on multiple occasions, the drama that I continuously found myself in, and me leaving a channel that was doing well to start a new one. I had found myself stuck in a pattern that whenever my life was going well and things were good, I would find a way to self-sabotage. I believe I would do so, so then I could find a reason to grind and work hard again and fight my way back up to the top.

When I flew to Australia on my first motivational speaking tour with my friend Adam Saleh who would be performing music from his albums that Spring, I was immediately disappointed when I noticed we were performing to audiences of maybe 350 people, night after night.

"There's something not right here," I said to Adam. "When I was completely new to the game I performed in front of 3,500 people here in Australia."

The only explanation was that the promotor had done a really bad job, which was underlined when fans would come up to me in the street, astonished that I was there. That convinced me to try to organize a show on my own.

Adam and I had a few free days after our final show in Australia, and we headed to a music studio in Melbourne so that Adam could work on his music. While we were there, I got bored and suddenly heard myself announce, "I'm going to write a song, it's going to be a diss track about RiceGum."

"Uh...OK?" The producer sounded skeptical.

RiceGum was huge on YouTube, the undisputed king of diss tracks at the time, and that's why I thought it would be a good idea to write a diss track about *him*—not to bring him down, but to use humor and love to bring an end to all the dissing. I wrote the song with a producer named Divy Pota and was *really* high as we recorded it. High to the point I was taking a total of three Adderalls a day and smoking weed simultaneously. It felt as if my heart was beating out of my chest, and at one point I found myself saying to Adam: "I'm about to faint. I feel like I'm going to die."

Despite that, I kept popping more Adderall, and the higher I got and the better I thought the song sounded, the more intense the thoughts about the show I was going to put on became.

"I just had an incredible idea!" I yelled over to Adam.

"Yeah?" he said.

"I'm gonna fly to LA, rent a massive venue, give out thousands of tickets on the street—or just sell them for twenty dollars apiece—and say, 'Hey, I'm doing this motivational show on July 15. Would you like to come?'"

"Really?" Adam replied, rolling his eyes.

"Yeah, I'll get artists to come and perform, but I'm going to be the headliner and deliver a motivational speech. One that will change the world and put an end to racism. And at the end, I'll debut my song on RiceGum and put an end to diss tracks." I was really losing it but no one knew I was abusing Adderall so they had no reason to doubt my judgment.

I went through to one of the other studio rooms and wrote "July 15" on the whiteboard. I took a picture and uploaded it to my Instagram Stories and twitter, then started posting more cryptic messages like, "July 15, Los Angeles. Be ready." The news was spreading all over the place, and people started asking, "What in the world is July 15?" The hype grew when I started tweeting pictures of huge crowds from places like Coachella, writing "This is what I want July 15 to look like."

This is where I made a decision that would change the course of my life forever. The two tour shows were done. All I had to do was fly back to New Jersey, wait one month, and then continue on the next leg of the tour internationally. But, here's where things took a turn. Instead of travelling back to my parents' house in

New Jersey as planned, I convinced Adam to fly to Los Angeles with me. We rented an Airbnb and had July 15 T-shirts made. I posted a video of me dancing in one of them, saying that something crazy was going to happen on that day. Not even I knew what was planned for that day.

I was still taking Adderall two or three times a day, but reality occasionally caught up with me, and I found myself thinking, *July 15 is only a week away, and I need to plan something huge. The only question is what.*

The first thing I did was call an old manager of mine and had him help me hire the Greek Theatre, an outdoor arena in Griffith Park. It cost $350,000, and I paid for it with my own money. There was no time to look for investors and I was keen on making this even successful. Over the next few days, I also managed to get Ticketmaster and Live Nation on board. I started calling every single person I knew—including people I had lost touch with—asking for their support. One of them—a guy who worked in the music industry—helped to book all the artists I wanted to perform at my show. Next thing I knew, I'd managed to line up some rappers from New York, LA, and Atlanta—some of the biggest names in the game. They all agreed to show up if I'd pay for their first-class tickets, their hotel rooms, and anything else they and their entourage wanted.

The next day, I announced that the show would be called "Hate Dies, Love Arrives," and more or less promised that it would lead to all hatred, prejudice, racism, and evil being wiped off the face of the earth. I was like a crazy person online, writing, "On July 15, I'm going to have more eyes on me than the President of the United States. I'm going to deliver a motivational speech that's going to change the world forever!"

Before long, every YouTuber was talking about the event, and though I didn't announce the artists who would be performing, I said, "Trust me, this is going to be a jam-packed night of music. This is going to be crazy."

I started tweeting every popular YouTuber I could, telling them that I needed them to show up, and they all said yes.

I had the venue, I'd given away 5,000 tickets for free online which were gone in minutes, I had a huge lineup of artists, and a bunch of famous YouTubers promising to show up. I also had a streaming service that would livestream the whole event on YouTube. Everything seemed to be going my way.

**"I'm battling with myself
and every day it's a war."**

—LUDACRIS

GOD'S POSITIONING SYSTEM

My manic phase reaches its peak.

The event was less than twenty-four hours away, and it was like electricity was in the air. I'd flown in all my childhood friends from the Bay Area and brought them to the Airbnb Adam and I were renting. I was high on Adderall again, and me and a couple of friends decided to go out to a restaurant to eat and celebrate. For a joke, I decided to hang my head out of the window of our Uber like Joker in *The Dark Knight*. I held up my phone and posted an Instagram story, screaming: "Yo, Drake, I heard you're in LA. Where you at? I need to invite you to July 15."

By the time we got to the restaurant, there was a paparazzo waiting for us outside. He immediately started filming me, and since I had just been joking about Drake on my Instagram story, I continued in the same vein. "Yo, tomorrow—July 15—I'm gonna deliver a motivational speech that will change the world. Drake, I need you there."

Once I was done and the paparazzo stopped recording, he told me, "I know where Drake is, you know."

"Where?"

He told us the name of the club, so instead of going into the restaurant to eat, the paparazzo and I exchanged numbers, and I jumped back into the Uber to head over there.

The only problem was that the bouncer shook his head when I asked whether Drake was inside. The whole evening suddenly felt like a huge failure.

Right then, the paparazzo called me. "Drake is at the Delilah, man. He rented the whole club."

We jumped back into the Uber and told the driver to take us to 7969 Santa Monica Boulevard, but when we got there, the doorman refused to let us in.

"This is a private event. Go home."

Feeling pissed, we turned back to the Uber. The thought of inviting Drake had taken hold, and it was all I could think about. I turned to my friends and said, "You guys can go home. I need to do this on my own."

They headed off, and at first, I didn't know what to do. That was when I remembered OVO Jonny, who owned the tattoo parlor where I'd gotten my Dollar and Muffin tattoo in Toronto when I was on tour with Roman Atwood. At that point I no longer felt I needed to take account of my parents' and my fans' expectations of me. I no longer made content catered to the Muslim or Middle Eastern audience. I felt like they had all turned their backs on me once I began living a Westernized LA lifestyle but I had felt like they had turned their backs on me. Over the course of a year I got a full half sleeve on my right arm and even tattooed a hairline on my head from a procedure called SMP. That's a whole other story on its own. Mama saw a picture of the tattoo that a fan tweeted her, and she called me when I was at the airport in Toronto to ask if it was really true. "Yes, Mama, it's true", I said, "but it doesn't mean I'm not your son anymore. I just wanna feel like I'm living *my* life." To my surprise, she understood me then and still accepted me as her son.

OVO Jonny's brother was Drake's best friend. I called him and explained the situation, asking whether he thought it was OK if I tried to track down Drake to invite him to the event or if it would make me look bad.

"Brother," he said, "I can't tell you what to do, but if God is telling you what to do, let him lead the way."

In the wound-up state I was in, his words sounded totally logical and obvious. At the time, I felt like God *was* leading the way. For some reason, during my manic phase, it was the closest I had ever felt to having a connection with God and my religion. I was praying five times a day. Making my friends pray alongside me and telling them that I wasn't the one making these things happen. God was. I was dripping with sweat, and my mouth was dry. It was like I was possessed, like something was making my arms and legs move, because before I knew it I was back in front of the doorman, trying to talk my way inside. Right as I was doing that, a young guy came over to me.

"Hey, my name is Show Luciano, but I go by Lit Papi," he said. "I was born in Los Angeles, but I don't want to die here. I know you're having a concert tomorrow. I'm an aspiring rapper, please put me on your stage."

I was in a manic state with one goal in mind, so I said, "Sure. Give me your phone number, and I'll hook you up with my team. You can be the first performer tomorrow."

"Thank you," he said with a smile, typing his number into my phone. "If you need anything from me, just let me know."

Lit Papi walked off, and I went 'round the corner into the club's parking lot where I found a guy and two girls who happened to be fans of mine.

"What are you guys doing?" I asked.

"Our friend is about to let us in through the side door," the guy told me.

"Can I come in with you?"

He shrugged. "Yeah."

Next thing I knew, the door opened, and I felt like I was being guided by a higher power as I walked in behind them. But I had barely made it inside before another doorman put a hand on my shoulder and said: "You ain't coming in tonight."

"But I'm with them," I said, nodding to my new friends.

"Yeah, they can come in, but you can't."

Just like that, I found myself back out front again.

That was when I spotted Lit Papi for a second time. He was standing in the smoking area behind a cage, and when he spotted me, he started waving his hand.

"Hey, come here!"

I went over to him.

"If you wanna come in, go 'round the back right now."

Since I still had a sense that there was a deeper purpose to everything that was happening, I did as he said and stood by what could only have been Drake's Rolls-Royce. His security guards were standing ten feet away from me, and they kept glancing over at me with a look as if I belonged there. But before they had time to realize I had no right being there, the rear door of the club flew open and Lit Papi waved me inside.

He led me through the hot, noisy kitchen and into the club. It was packed, and Lit Papi turned to me and said, "Every celebrity you can think of is in here tonight." He quickly reeled off a long list of huge names, ending with, "Drake!"

It was like a bolt of electricity shot through my body. "Drake," I said. "How do I find Drake?"

Lit Papi gave me a mysterious smile and said, "GPS."

"What's that?"

"God's positioning system. Let God lead the way."

My jaw dropped because that was exactly what OVO Jonny had just told me on the phone.

With that, Lit Papi turned and walked away.

For a split second I panicked because I couldn't see anyone I knew in there. I had no money and no ID, and I'd already been kicked out once. I was also dehydrated as hell because of all the Adderall I'd taken, and I had no plan of action. For the longest time, I just stood there. My feet wouldn't move. I posted a picture of my motionless feet on Instagram and wrote, "I'm meeting Drake tonight."

What happened next, I will never be able to explain and very few people in life will ever believe. Every step I took inside the club was not by my doing. My legs were operating on their own. The words coming out of my mouth were coming out on their own. I was not in control of my body. Right then, I felt an almost overwhelming sense of being on a divine mission, so I started moving from one celebrity to another, reeling off the details like a mantra: "Tomorrow, on July 15, I'm gonna throw an event that will change the world." I didn't care whether they looked uncomfortable or uninterested. It was like a higher power was guiding me, putting me into the right position. That's why I wasn't at all surprised to find myself sitting at a table with Ludacris, telling him all about what was happening the next day. More accurately: screaming in his face because the music was so loud. Don't get me wrong, it was a pretty big deal to be talking with Ludacris, but the only person I really cared about finding was Drake, and I couldn't see him anywhere.

It wasn't until people started heading home that I managed to find his entourage in a quiet area of the club, and I froze, because I recognized an older guy who walked right by me—Drake's father, a guy I had met and spoken to at the premiere of Tyler Perry's *Boo! A Madea Halloween*.

I stopped him and started reeling off my speech about the event but quickly realized he was way too tipsy to understand a word I was saying.

He staggered off, and I reflexively reached out to stop him from falling. My hand accidentally brushed the gentlemen guiding him from behind instead, and he turned and looked at me.

I'd never seen him before, but that didn't stop me from telling my story again. I ended with the words, "I'm gonna be the next Tony Robbins. The only difference is that my name is Yousef Saleh Erakat."

He stared at me for a moment, then laughed and said, "Wow, I love everything you just said, but I have one question. How did you know my name?"

I had no memory of saying his name, so I replied, "I swear, I've never met you or seen you before in my life. If your name just came out of my mouth, God did that."

"Wow," he said again, before walking over to the group around Drake. The crowd seemed to part as he approached, allowing him to walk straight through to someone—Drake.

I felt my heart racing. This was the first time the whole night that I was in eye sight of Drake. What started out as a joke with me hanging my head outside of an Uber had turned into reality. The guy I'd just been speaking to leaned into Drake and said something, pointing back toward me.

It was like a bright light was shining straight at me, and I was filled with an energy I'd never experienced before, something I couldn't control. I felt icy cold one minute, red hot the next, and I thought, *Oh my God, I did it!*

The guy started walking back over with Drake right behind him.

They stopped in front of me. Drake was so close that we were practically standing face-to-face. He wasn't looking at me; he was focused on the NBA player he was shaking hands with and saying goodbye to. Somehow, I managed to restrain myself from interrupting him to ask what I'd come to ask. I stood perfectly still instead, barely daring to breathe until Drake took a step forward and walked away.

His friend came up to me a moment later and said, "We'll be there tomorrow. Here's my number. Text me all the details." I saved his number under Drake's hit song, "God's Plan."

I left the club not long later, so high I was shaking all over. I took an Uber back to the Airbnb, and when my girlfriend opened the door, I said, "Don't touch me right now. There's an energy inside me, and I don't know what it is. Tell everyone to come downstairs and wait for me."

Without another word, I went upstairs and got into the shower. I dropped to my knees and raised my face, letting the water wash down over me until I felt composed enough to talk. It was as if a spirit was leaving my body. I feel as though I was possessed. Looking back now, I still feel as if I was, but not by a good spirit.

With nothing but a towel wrapped around my hips, I went back down to see my friends, who had gathered like my girlfriend told them to. They all turned to me with curious faces as I sat down with my legs crossed and told them what I'd been through that evening. I rounded off the whole story by announcing:

"So, Drake's gonna be there tomorrow."

"You have to jump into disaster
with both feet."

—CHUCK PALAHNIUK

JULY 15

My life is torn to shreds.

The next morning, once I had convinced myself it wasn't all a dream, I broke the news on Twitter and Instagram. I posted a picture of Drake, hyping up the show with promises that he'd be there.

I sent the same image to the number Drake's friend had given me. I wanted to show him I was doing all I could to promote Drake's involvement in the show. He didn't reply, but the fact that each text I sent him said "read" showed me that I had their approval. If I didn't he would have surely texted me to tell me to stop before they sent me a cease and desist. I mean announcing Drake at an event isn't a small deal.

Filled with the most insane belief that I would soon be performing the biggest manifestation of life that anyone had ever seen, I walked barefoot around the garden behind the hotel that my girlfriend and I had checked into because the Airbnb had gotten a bit too chaotic. I was reeling off improvised prayers. Or I did until my phone beeped, distracting me. It was a direct message from a YouTuber who was more of an enemy than a friend, best known for the fact that his fans would sabotage his livestreams by calling in anonymous threats to the establishments he was at. Doxing is what it's called. He asked if he could come to my event, and because of the state of mind I was in, I decided to be generous: "Brother, this event is all about putting a stop to all the hate and bringing out the positive, so of course, you can come."

Not long later, I got a call from the guy who was helping me arrange the whole event. He said, "Hey, just to let you know, Ticketmaster and Live Nation say that if this goes well, they'll have a $2 million advance to give you for the next one."

I truly believed that I'd created the next Coachella.

The preparations were in full swing over at the Greek Theatre. The audience had begun to arrive, and all the artists and YouTubers who would be performing had been gathered backstage for some time. By the time I jumped into an Uber to head over there, the event had already begun. As the pre-show started and Lit Papi was performing on stage, there were 71,000 people watching live on YouTube, before the night even kicked off.

Sitting in the car—after popping another Adderall—everything felt magical. Or it did until I got a call from my girlfriend.

In floods of tears, she said, "Someone called in a bomb threat to the theater, so the event has been cancelled."

In that split second, everything changed. My life had been altered forever. Suddenly I was no longer on my way to what I had thought would be the high point of my life—an event the entire internet was watching—but to the beginning of my downfall.

I stared blankly ahead, trying to work out how to say the things I wanted to say, the words I had practiced over and over. But when we arrived at the Greek Theatre, I couldn't think of anything better to do than ask my friends inside the theater to tell everyone to gather on the grass parking lot outside, where I had just jumped out of the car. Before long there were thousands of people around me, and I turned to my Uber driver, "Can my friends and I get on the roof of the car? I'll buy you a new one and give you $50,000 if you let me."

The driver shrugged. "Sure, go for it."

I climbed up on the roof and started talking, actually screaming, without a megaphone, to everyone who was gathered in the parking lot.

The sense of calm I'd felt earlier was gone. I was manic, on an Adderall high and determined to take my revenge on the cruel fate that wanted to ruin things for me. I gestured wildly and screamed what I had planned to say from the stage, but I looked like I was crazy. To be fair and honest with myself for the first time, I was crazy. I spotted a fellow YouTuber in the crowd who ran one of the biggest drama channels on the site. He was standing there with a huge camera and his entire crew filming an entire documentary on my event, and I felt my stomach turn.

"Yo," he shouted. "Was this whole event just for you to put out a diss track about RiceGum?"

The track had been mistakenly released on iTunes at midnight the night before the event. It was a shame because I had been planning to go out on stage *with* RiceGum and say something along the lines of, "I'm sick of everybody roasting each other, so I made the diss track to end all diss tracks. I'm gonna perform that shit live. Here we go!"

In the moment, that felt impossible to explain, so instead I just yelled, "Fuck you! You ruined my life for years! You made me want to kill myself!"

He had long been targeting me on his channel when I was at the top of my game, and he seemed to be enjoying himself. I saw him smile before I turned away and kept on yelling the things I had been planning to say, talking about everything from racial injustice to the Palestinian freedom struggle.

As I shouted myself hoarse on top of the car, and only audible to the people standing closest to me, police helicopters circled overhead, and three news vans pulled into the parking lot to record everything. It was the most attention I'd ever had, but I didn't give a single thought to how I must look. I just didn't want to accept that it had all gone to shit.

I started to worry that my more political statements might piss off people at the very top of politics and the military. I became convinced they would lock me up and execute me, and in a state of panic I slumped onto the roof of the car in tears.

My bodyguard 'Country' who was always by my side since the Roman Vs Fousey Tour, and who was like a brother to me, came forward and said, "It's time to go home now."

He helped me down from the roof of the car, climbed into the back seat beside me, and told the driver to go. I was still sobbing, so exhausted that I could barely even look up at all of the silent faces staring at me through the window.

"If they don't know your dreams,
then they can't shoot them down."

—J. COLE

THE LAUGHING STOCK
OF THE INTERNET

I make a new promise.

The next day, of course, a bunch of journalists got in touch. They could barely hide their glee as they asked me to explain what went wrong. I answered as best I could, but quickly realized that all they really wanted to know was whether Drake had actually promised to come.

"Were you really standing face-to-face with him?" one journalist asked me. I replied "yes," but he had already decided I was lying. Drake's team had put out a statement claiming that they had no idea who I was and had no intentions of ever being a part of the event.

I was the biggest laughing stock online, and the frustration I felt made me completely lose control. Just take the interview I agreed to with the same YouTuber making a documentary on me a couple of days later.

He and I already had a tense relationship, as I said earlier, and I was still convinced that he'd come to the Greek Theatre with his team in the hope that the whole event would be a fiasco.

As a result, I should have just ignored him when he called and said he wanted to give me the opportunity to share my side of the story. Instead, I got into the car with a couple friends and drove over to the house he was staying at in LA, the Clout House.

Suddenly, and for no reason at all, I asked one of my friends to record a video of me on his phone.

As soon as he started recording, I said, "Guys, just to prove to you how real the law of attraction is, the next time J. Cole performs at the STAPLES Center, I will be front row at his concert and I will actually walk out on stage barefoot with a picture of Dollar on my shirt and introduce him, perform my speech, and start the concert. And if I'm not, I swear I'll quit the internet for good. I'll give my channels away; I'll kill my social media accounts and leave the country!" Why I said that and where that came from I may never know.

The interview with Keemstar was a disaster from the very start. The fact I was still manic and high on Adderall meant certain words came flooding out of me including my promise to introduce J. Cole at the STAPLES Center. After just the first or second question, I got all emotional and started crying and screaming, and I realized later that a lot of the people listening were worried about me while the other half were laughing at me with pure hatred toward me convinced I was evil. The narrative had become that I was manipulative, a liar, a con artist, delusional, narcissistic, and even that I had called in the bomb threat on myself because I knew that Drake was never going to show up.

The very next day, I called Adam Saleh and said I couldn't go on with the rest of the tour with him. I explained that if I didn't do what I had promised in presenting J. Cole at the STAPLES Center, I would be the biggest laughing stock on the internet. Adam said he understood, and we ended the call as friends. Then I bought front row tickets to five J. Cole shows, including the concert at the STAPLES Center in August. I had to fly across the United States to the first show, and to my disappointment I didn't manage to get close to J. Cole or any of his crew. The same happened at the next gig. After the third show, I stayed behind in the arena with my girlfriend. Fans were bombarding me asking for pictures. Eventually, one of the security guards came up to me and said, "Come on, let's go out the back entrance."

I squeezed my girlfriend's hand. "See, everything happens like God wants it to."

We followed the security guard a few meters, then I stopped and said to him, "Hold on.... Just listen to what I have to say."

I explained all about my meeting with Drake and the show that had imploded on July 15, telling him how important it was that I meet J. Cole.

"Wow," he said. "Take my number. We can talk."

At first, I didn't really know what to think, but after sending a few messages back and forth the next day, it felt like I might be able to keep the promise I'd made after all.

The next J. Cole concert was in San Diego, but I'd given away my front row tickets to a fan on Instagram. I bought the next best tickets I could. That meant my girlfriend and I were sitting pretty far back in the arena, but when I turned around and saw the DJ booth, I had an idea.

"Wait here," I told my girlfriend.

I walked over to two empty seats right by the booth. My girlfriend didn't understand what I was doing.

"These seats are way worse."

I just nodded to the DJ booth. "You see those guys? They're J. Cole's crew." The two guys who the seats had belonged to came up to me with an attitude and demanded I get out of their seats. I had explained to them that if they took the better seats in front of these where I was originally sitting, I would pay them an extra $1,500. They agreed. During an intermission I had took them to the bar, bought them drinks, and told them about the mission I was on.

Being the huge J. Cole fan I was, I recognized everyone around in the DJ booth, and once the show was over I walked right up to them. The first person I saw was one of J. Cole's first producers, Elite.

I held out a hand to him, and as we chatted I noticed another guy in the booth. He was looking at me, and after a few fans asked for my picture, he came over and spoke to me.

Something told me this was the moment I had been waiting for, and I started telling him about what had happened on July 15 and why I wanted to introduce J. Cole at the STAPLES Center.

"To get your message out?"

I nodded.

He pulled out his phone, and I realized that the wallpaper was a picture of him and J. Cole as kids. I thought "Oh my God, this must be his childhood friend."

He took my number and then walked off.

I turned to my girlfriend and said, "See, God's leading the way."

I was still totally convinced it would happen when I turned up at the STAPLES Center in Los Angeles two days later—blood full of Adderall, like usual—even though J. Cole's childhood friend hadn't been in touch and his security guard hadn't replied to any of my messages.

I was wearing a T-shirt with a picture of my dog, Dollar, on it, and slippers so I could be barefoot on stage. The minute I stepped into the arena, I felt a kind of electricity, an expectation. I thought, *this is it.*

I tried not to think about everything that was at stake: my YouTube channels, my career, my place in the country, and to be quite honest, my entire existence.

I walked past the DJ booth but couldn't see his childhood friend anywhere in sight. Instead, I tried to call the security guard, but he didn't pick up. Still filled with confidence, I decided to walk up to another security guard. But when I asked him about his colleague, he shook his head.

"He got called to a different show today, so it's me instead. What's up?"

It was like a cold wind started blowing through the arena.

"Fuck!" I shouted. I told him everything, speaking way too fast, and rounded off with what I needed to do that evening.

He stared at me with a sad look on his broad, slightly scarred face.

"I'm sorry," he said. "I don't know you, so that's not happening tonight. Besides, Cole wouldn't want anyone near his stage."

I walked back to my seat in the front row as though in a haze.

Still, it wasn't until J. Cole walked out onto the stage that I finally realized what I'd done to my life. This was the end.

"Success on the outside means nothing unless you also have success within."

—ROBIN SHARMA,
THE MONK WHO SOLD HIS FERRARI

THE MOST HATED MAN
ON THE INTERNET

My friends turn their backs on me, and I feel like smashing my head through a window.

My memories of the days that followed are totally hazy. Within the space of just a few weeks, I'd lost *everything*. Not only the $1 million I'd spent on an event that had been canceled due to a bomb threat but also my identity, which was completely bound up in what I did on my channels: my self-respect, self-love, identity, personality, humor, love, life. I was an empty vessel without a soul. I felt empty. I no longer knew who I was. I had made a public pledge never to show my face on the internet again. The only problem was that my promised absence didn't seem to have done anything to stop people's need to spew bile about me. "You're the biggest narcissistic liar!" one person wrote. "I hope you kill yourself," said someone else. At the worst point, one of my friends tried to delete all the comments as they came in, but there were literally thousands of them coming in every couple of minutes. It was nonstop.

In order to keep my promise, I offered to let one of my friends take over my Twitch channel and split the profit with him. I gave away one of my YouTube channels to a friend on the same terms. "You can change it to your name and post whatever you want," I told him. I gave the other YouTube channel to my trusty camera guy, Ali Baluch and gave my main 10 million subscriber channel away to the FANS, telling them they could email me and I'll upload any video they want on the channel and deleted my Twitter, Instagram, and Facebook accounts.

The only problem was that I had no idea what to do next, and the stress of that made me feel even worse. So I booked a week's getaway for myself at the Shambhala Mountain Center at Red Feather Lakes, Colorado, where I had no access to either my phone or internet. Every day there was meditation at 5:00 AM, 1:00 PM, and 8:00 PM, with healthy meals in between. The reason I went to Shambhala Mountain Center was that I had just read *The Monk Who Sold His Ferrari* and felt I was in the same situation as the main protagonist in the book. I was hoping to meet a monk who could help me find a new way of living, and who I could unburden my heart to. I wanted to leave my old lifestyle in the past. Let go of all materialistic possessions and find the true essence of existence. And one day when I was on my way to morning meditation, I really did catch sight of a monk and said, "Have you got time to meet me later...? I'd like to tell you my story."

He fixed his eyes on me and said calmly: "Of course."

We went for a walk later that day and I told him every single thing that had happened over the last couple of months. When I was done, we sat down on a bench and he looked at me without blinking for what felt like more than five minutes. Then he took several deep breaths and said, "This too shall pass. There's a reason for all the things that have happened to you."

I remember feeling disappointed, because that left me none the wiser. More than anything, I felt just as lost when I left Shambhala Mountain Center as I had when I arrived.

My girlfriend could see that I was still suffering and quickly booked a getaway for the two of us outside of Los Angeles the minute I got back.

But as we drove out there the next day, I was so sick with stress and worries that we soon had to pull over to the side of the road so I could throw up. And we had only just arrived at the resort when the next bad thing happened: a good friend of mine started posting YouTube videos full of false information about me, even going so far as to say things like I was a manipulative psycho for thinking I could pull off an event like July 15, and that I gave my girlfriend Stockholm syndrome during the process.

It really hurt me. And I couldn't defend myself because I'd gotten rid of all my channels and left social media. I had no place to speak or share my side of the story and even if I did, the entire internet despised me. No one would listen.

I literally felt like I was suffocating. I couldn't breathe; I couldn't speak; and I started crying so hard that my entire body shook. After an hour or two of that in our suite, I looked up at my girlfriend and said, "I'm booking a flight to Bali. I need to leave the country for good."

JOURNAL

October 7th

Today was possibly the hardest day of my life. I've reached a point where suicide makes sense. I was supposed to be in Ojai right now, spending a night out with my girlfriend. But instead, to Bali. And boy, am I scared. Terrified, actually. So many fear-based questions that I wish I knew the answers to. How long am I going for? Where am I going? How will I feel when I get there? The list goes on and on. But I think the beauty is not knowing any of the answers and having to deal with them as they arise. As of right now, I don't know what the future has in store for me, and I don't know if I'm doing the right thing. But I'm doing it with full faith that by changing my frequency and vibrations today, it'll shape a better tomorrow. God is the greatest of all time. And I have to remember that it's better to be alone than to be in the company of those that do not deserve me. I have my girlfriend, my dog, my mama, baba, and siblings. The rest can come and go as they please.

It was evening when I landed in Denpasar, and it was hot. At least one hundred degrees. All I'd taken with me was $10,000 in cash and a rucksack containing a few shorts and T-shirts.

With some kind of tunnel vision and a billion thoughts swirling around my head, I climbed into one of the cabs waiting outside the terminal building and headed straight for the Goddess Retreat, where I'd booked a suite with my own pool and back-yard for an unspecified amount of time. You'd be surprised at how cheap it was to live this way in Bali.

I remember falling asleep almost as soon as I lay down on the bed after checking in. I slept dreamlessly that night, and when I woke up at sunrise the next morning, I decided to go for a run.

The dawn light was just starting to creep down the mountains surrounding the resort, and as I ran along the busy streets, it was amazingly beautiful.

The minute I felt my anxiety creeping up on me, I sped up. I kept doing that until my entire being was reduced to nothing but breathing and my heartbeat.

A few hours later, when I was back at the hotel, I had some coffee and ate banana pancakes, then jumped into the pool (the water was pretty much body temperature) for a long swim. After that, I lay down by the pool side and meditated in the sun for a while before I picked up the book *The Monk Who Sold His Ferrari*, which fit my life perfectly—for that reason, I wanted to reread it.

October 10th

WELL, I did it! I'm writing this from mother effin' BALI! WOOO-OOOOO! This is only day one, but the transformation already feels HUGE. I know I made the right move. I believe it with every fiber in my body! This was one small step that will provide so much growth and change in my life, moving it in the direction I want to go in. Is it easy? Hell no. I'm all alone in a private resort in a country thousands of miles away from where I find my comfort. But it's sure as hell going to be worth it.

Today I woke up at 5:00 AM, went for a run, ate breakfast, meditated, handled a bunch of calls, and it's STILL only 9:00 AM! THAT IS INSANE! I love myself. I love my family. I LOVE MUFFIN. I LOVE LIFE. I could not be happier right now. (Well, that's a bit optimistic, I'm sure I could, but this attitude will help me get there.)

October 11th

Today was interesting to say the least. I'm following a "morning routine" that helps me get up and start my day with a nice KICK, but soon after I'm done, my day slowly begins to unravel.

My ego and anxiety are two big components in my life at the moment. My ego furiously tries to find ways to show itself. Planning, planning, and planning to get back into the public eye. Like an annoying kid running wild in my head all day long. Do this! Do that! Do this and that! It never ends. I also fear and worry about the future a lot. I tend to skip ahead to later in life, but I'm accessing that time as my current self. I don't take into consideration that when the future I'm visualizing and fantasizing about really arrives, I'll be a completely different person. So my thoughts and feelings toward the future are pretty much null and void.

I'm going to stop writing now because my anxiety is getting too much. I'll be back tomorrow.

October 13th

Yesterday was a hard day, like nothing I've ever experienced before. The stress of everything got so much that my legs were shaking intensely, and I had trouble even lifting them off the ground. On top of that, my neck felt really stiff. Horrible feeling! I was sitting in a café when it started, and I had an urge to grab my stuff and run back to the retreat, but I also knew that in the state I was in, I wouldn't be able to walk a single mile. Instead, I packed up my things and dragged myself across the street to the spa on the other side.

Once I'd paid and gone down to the spa area, I spotted a girl and started talking to her. In some weird sense, it was like talking to myself. Her life story and problems, the stresses and anxiety she had.... Everything she said was something I could identify with in my very core. I gave it a shot and started opening up to her, little by little. And sure enough, it was like the answers and advice she gave me were straight out of the books I'd been reading lately. We spoke for hours, and after jumping into the cold bath several times—a question of mind over matter—I came back to the retreat and got into bed. I had my first good sleep in quite some time.

October 15th (11:25 AM)

It's crazy, because it feels like so much time has passed (so much has happened), but when I check my diary I realize I'm only twelve days into this spiritual journey. There's a sense of relief in that.

No one has the power or ability to diminish my light. Not even if the whole world were to stand against me. Being alone with God (away from the love I have from my family and good friends) is a beautiful feeling. I use each moment as an opportunity to grow, to learn, and to become a better version of myself. I'm twelve days into my new life, and I'm already starting to feel better. We set the limitations in our lives. We create the mental road blocks. We control our destiny through God. This IS only the beginning. I will rise, as I have proved to myself time and time again. Alhamdulillah. Alhamdulillah. Alhamdulillah.

At that point in time, I was somehow still convinced I could get out of the situation I found myself in. In fact, it wasn't until my friend started posting more and more videos about me that I understood just how close to the surface my panicked anxiety had been all along. It was a calculated attack on my character to eradicate and end me while I was already down. I realized I needed people around me, so I left the resort and headed to a yoga retreat instead, booking myself in for a week.

On my very first night there, the yoga instructor gathered all the new arrivals in a circle on the floor.

"I'd like you to introduce yourselves, one by one, and tell everyone why you're here."

As I peered around the group, I noticed that I was the only man there. I was surrounded by middle aged Western women who were saying things like, "I want to learn more about both yoga and myself so I can be even happier in life." When my turn came 'round, I immediately started to cry. No one said a word until I broke the silence.

"I'm going through the worst period of my life," I said. "I no longer want to be alive. I have no more purpose. I don't know what I'm doing, so I'm hoping this trip will save me or give me some sort of enlightenment."

A few days later, I must have eaten something bad at dinner, because I got really sick. I woke in the middle of the night, vomiting violently. Before long, I was also suffering from absurdly explosive diarrhea. I dragged myself from my room the next morning, and turned to the group: "I'm sorry guys, but I can't go out with you today."

I went straight back to my bathroom and continued to throw up. In the middle of that whole sorry story, I also started talking with my girlfriend over the phone. I ended up getting extremely upset again about those videos my friend had posted, and I completely lost it and yelled, "You know what? I'm going to fucking end it all once and for all!"

A moment later, I broke the window with my head, then passed out on the bed with blood all over my face.

When I woke up again I had no idea how many hours—days—I had been lying in the fetal position in bed. Not until one evening when there was a knock at the door.

It was my yoga instructor, and she came into the room with another woman who worked as a psychologist at the retreat.

The instructor sat down next to me on the bed and gave me a pitying look.

WARNING

"Yousef, with love, we feel that you're mentally unfit to be here right now. We think it would be best if you went home to your family."

October 20th (6:09 PM)

I feel empty. I feel lost. I feel like I have no spirit or soul or heart or brain. I feel broken. I feel unhappy. I have no source of real happiness. I feel anger. I feel guilt. I regret giving away my YouTube channels and wish I could get them back. I feel like everyone hates me.

"In Hollywood if you don't have a shrink, people think you're crazy."

—JOHNNY CARSON

OFF THE INTERNET

I get stuck in customs and find a therapist
in New Jersey who seems to be able to help me.

By this point, Mama and Baba had sold our childhood home in Fremont and used the money to move to San Diego. They no longer wanted to live in New Jersey since I had left and Mama had always wanted to be closer to her mom, who lived there. Throughout my childhood, I remember her saying, "We're moving to San Diego next year." This happened every single year of my childhood but she never pulled the trigger. This was her first time making her lifelong dream a reality.

Since I had often gone to San Diego to visit my grandmother, and because my parents were now living there, it felt like the right place to go. Or it did until I got to customs at the airport and stood by one of the automated machines answering what felt like an endless line of boring questions. One of them asked whether I was bringing more than a certain amount of money with me into the country, and without really thinking about what I was doing, I hit the no button.

The problem was the $10,000 I had in my backpack. I had barely spent any of it in Bali and had most of it still with me.

As I passed through security, I was asked to follow a TSA officer into a bare interview room and told to sit down on one side of an empty table.

The officer, a sturdy, middle-aged man, gave me a wary look and started asking questions as though I was a criminal. I noticed how glassy-eyed I became and knew how guilty I must look. Things didn't get any better when a police officer came into the room and sat down beside the TSA officer, asking questions that suggested my money came from selling drugs in foreign countries.

The whole situation was so unpleasant and unsettling that I started to cry. I eventually managed to sob, "You have to believe me, I'm not a drug dealer! I just took that money with me so I could start a new life in Bali. My life here is over. Please don't take my money, it's all I've got left."

My voice broke and I sobbed uncontrollably.

"I'm sorry," I bawled. "I'm sorry; I'm sorry."

The police officer squirmed.

"Listen kid, I don't know what you're going through, but I swear you'll get through this. We're not going to take your money, but you're gonna get a fine."

"Thank you. Thank you," I said, wiping my nose with the back of my hand.

The two officers got up and showed me out into the arrivals hall, where Mama and Baba were waiting for me.

They both seemed shocked when they saw me, probably because I'd lost so much weight during my time in Bali. My eyes were hollow, my face had lost all of its light and the vibrant smile I once had that could light up an entire room was gone. I looked sick in every sense, and as Mama hugged me, she started to cry.

I woke at around twelve o'clock the next day, in the room my parents had made up for me in their house by Lake Murray, and went straight down to the kitchen. I noticed right away that my parents had decided that day would be like any other.

Mama smiled at me and said, "So, what do you want to do today?"

Baba looked up at me from his paper, giving me an encouraging smile.

There was no way I could play along with them; I was nothing but an empty shell. So I said, "I just want to stay home. My life's over anyway."

They exchanged a concerned glance but didn't try to convince me to join them when they went out for groceries a few hours later. All Mama said was, "You get some rest. Maybe you'll feel like doing something later."

I shrugged and went through to the lounge to lay down on the couch. I started watching a Netflix show but couldn't concentrate. My mind was still whirring, and one of the thoughts going 'round and 'round had to do with the fact that I couldn't accept my new reality as it was. I had lost everything—the fame, the money, my channels, my future. It felt like I'd had an arm or a leg amputated, and I soon started to hyperventilate and sweat. Seconds felt like minutes and minutes felt like hours. Not even thirty minutes had passed when my parents had returned home.

After what felt like an eternity, Mama opened the front door and shouted, "Yousef, we're home. Everything OK?" I was in the middle of a full-blown panic attack.

I realized just how serious it was when I saw Mama's face as she came into the living room.

"Are you OK!?"

"No," I said. "I need to go see a doctor."

Mama drove me to the nearest hospital, where I was taken to a brightly lit room in the psych ward. But rather than seeing a therapist or psychiatrist who could talk to me and prescribe me something to calm down, I had to lay on a bed for hours, dressed in a hospital gown and with Mama in the seat beside me. I kept repeating things like, "Mama, things will never be the same again.

You've lost your son. I'm a failure. There is no more life for me to live. My life is over."

Eventually the door opened and a doctor came into the room. She gave me a slightly harried glance and said, "So... what's the issue?"

I shook my head. "I don't even know where to begin. My life is over."

The doctor frowned and asked me a couple questions. My answers didn't cover even a fraction of everything I was feeling.

"Hmm," she said, turning to Mama. "Do you want him to stay so we can check on him and make sure he doesn't harm himself or do you want us to send him home?"

Mama wiped a couple of tears away. She looked like she was at a complete loss—which was totally understandable. She just wanted the best for me, but how was she supposed to know what that was?

The doctor sighed. "Well, think about it. I'll be back soon," she said with an impatient tone. With that, she turned and left the room.

The minute the door closed, I started crying. I turned to Mama, "I don't want to stay here. It'll cost so much money, and they're not gonna do anything. I just want to go home."

So, after being prescribed some sedatives, we drove back home.

My parents didn't stop trying to get me out of the house, and just a few days later they managed to convince me to go down to the beach with them.

The problem was that the entire internet had thought I was in Bali, off the internet, and never to be seen again. So I slumped down in the back seat with my sunglasses on the whole way to the big parking lot by the beach. As soon as we arrived to park, a group of five girls spotted me the minute Baba opened the driver-side door.

"Oh my God, it's Fousey!" they screamed, running over to us. "Can we get a picture?"

I felt sick and dizzy and immediately broke into a panic attack, "They're gonna tell everybody I'm back in the States! Everyone's gonna think I'm a liar." I started yelling at the top of my lungs, "Drive, Baba! Drive!"

Baba gave Mama an uncertain glance. She looked about as confused as he did. But then he closed the door and started the engine.

The minute we got back to the house, I went straight to my room and threw myself onto the bed. I refused to leave the house for quite some time after that—until one day when Baba asked me to come to the kitchen.

He and Mama were sitting at the table when I came into the room, and as I sat down opposite them they explained that they thought it would be best if we all returned to the house I'd bought them in New Jersey. I'd be able to move around outside more freely there.

I didn't have anything against the idea, so a week or two later we swapped the west coast for the east coast, where my oldest brother Mohammed also lived. As far as I was concerned, that was great, because I needed all the support I could get. My other siblings, Ahmed and Noura, also came to visit and did what they could to support me and talk some sense into me. Noura would sit me down and make posters for me where I would write what I was grateful for, what I wanted for my future, amongst other things. Ahmed would talk to me and provide books for me to read on how to let go of the past and how everything was going to be better. It made no difference.

In the end I managed to find a therapist right there in New Jersey and booked my first session with him.

The minute I got to his office, I had a bad feeling. For one, the tiny room smelled awful, and there were books and papers everywhere. The therapist—an old, grey-haired dude in a ratty jacket with dandruff on the shoulders—didn't really inspire much confidence either.

Despite that, I decided to give him a chance and started telling him about everything that happened around July 15. But before I had finished, he interrupted me and said, "Listen, man. I've had multi-millionaires in my office before; they lost everything, but they got it all back. You have nothing to cry about. You're fine." There was no sense of empathy or compassion toward anything I had shared or gone through.

For the first time since stepping into his room, I looked him in the eye.

I told him, "I'll pay for the whole hour, but I don't want to continue these sessions with you."

That really annoyed him, and we quickly got into an argument. The whole thing ended abruptly when I got to my feet and walked out.

Thankfully, I soon found another therapist who seemed both sensible and smart. She also really understood where I was coming from and got me to accept that it would be a long, bumpy road before I had any chance of feeling better. It was also covered by my insurance so I could go in on a daily basis. Every session was more or less the same. I would start with explaining the anxiety I felt waking up that morning, the nightmare I had during my sleep and how my life was over and there was nothing left for me to live for.

Back home, Mama and Baba were eager to see me make progress. Every time I came home from a therapy session, they would ask, "So are you feeling better now?"

I understood that they were worried and that they meant well, but I didn't want to lie to them anymore, so I always just replied, "No, that's not how therapy works."

There were times when they could see for themselves just how far I had to go. Like the day Baba came down to the basement and found me on all fours, crying my eyes out as I punched the floor as hard as I could. He had never seen me in that kind of state before, and the sight must really have shaken him because he sounded almost afraid as he asked me, "Yousef, what's happening?"

"Baba, my life is over," I howled, still punching the floor.

Without another word, he turned around and hurried back up the stairs. We never talked about what happened that day.

"I often stood in front of the mirror alone,
wondering how ugly a person could get."

—CHARLES BUKOWSKI

THE UGLIEST PERSON ON EARTH

I try to figure out how to make a comeback.

"There's something on your mind, Yousef," Mama said to me in the kitchen one morning. "What is it?"

At first I was shocked, because Mama had never talked to me that way before. For the first time in my life, I was able to look at my mama as a friend and confide in her. She had seen me at my worst and there was nothing left to hide. I just sighed and told her the truth. The good thing was that she took it so well, despite me revealing dark thoughts that would have terrified any parent. She would always remind me of this simple fact. "Yousef, you didn't harm anyone, you didn't hurt anyone, the only person whose life you affected is your own. You have no one to be sorry to."

She and I had really grown close while I was hiding from the world in that basement in New Jersey. I could also see just how much she was suffering whenever I started crying about having ruined my life and not knowing who I was anymore. My persona was in tatters, and that left me with a real identity crisis. Because if I wasn't Fousey, who was I?

The biggest problem was that the therapy sessions weren't helping me feel any better. I was still suffering with anxiety and fear, and that meant I started to hate my appearance even more than I had in the past. The worse I felt on the inside, the worse I felt on the outside. I would spend so long standing in front of the mirror in the bathroom, staring at my reflection. I decided that I had a disgustingly big nose, that my eyebrows were a weird shape, that my forehead was shiny. In my eyes, I really was the ugliest person on earth. The feelings I had of myself on the inside changed the way I saw myself on the outside.

That was why I felt such a mix of amazement and gratitude that my girlfriend still wanted me. The truth is that she was the only person left from my old life, and she was also my only remaining link to Los Angeles, where I no longer had an apartment, friends, or career. So I clung to her, the same way I clung to the thought of getting my old life back. The problem was that it didn't matter what I did, because any thoughts about making a comeback never led anywhere, and seemed to slip straight through my fingers.

I would secretly fly to Los Angeles and spend time with her for days at a time. The problem was I had no purpose. No reason to wake up in the morning and no reason to live. There was nothing on my agenda or to-do list. I would walk around the apartment mindlessly thinking of ways to fix the mess that I had created. At the same time, I was experimenting with different medications my psych would prescribe me. Each medicine came with a welcome period of side effects and they would make things all the worse. One for example, waking up at 6:00 AM every morning no matter how early or late I went to sleep and unable to feel my legs. The minute I would wake up, I would find myself in an anxiety attack.

It was like a curse. I would have a new anxiety attack at roughly the same time every afternoon as well, a direct consequence of my inability to do anything about my situation. And as soon as the clock struck seven, I would start drinking wine just to be able to cope.

One day around this time, I was invited onto Logan Paul's Impaulsive podcast. It was the first time in what felt like an eternity that I'd done anything online, and I remember how nervous

I was as I sat there trying to explain how everything had gone to shit. I wasn't trying to pass the buck in any way, though that was how some listeners interpreted it when I talked about having a manic period and not being in the right frame of mind at the time of the event.

I knew from past experience that people often thought I was making things up when it came to my mental health, and that became increasingly clear as soon as the podcast was released. Many of the comments claimed I was a manipulative liar, and there were also a bunch of jokes about Drake and July 15. But to my surprise, the vast majority of the comments were positive. People started writing things like, "It's good to see he's doing a little better."

That was enough to make me want to kickstart my career again, and when I reached out to my friends to tell them this, they immediately gave me my channels back. One of them did so because he knew that I knew he had stolen $15,000 from my account while I was in Bali and had no choice, another because he wasn't looking after the channel and realized being internet famous wasn't as easy as it seems, and the third because he thought it was my channel and that I should have it back, Ali Baluch.

I posted my first vlog back on my old vlogging channel, DOSEofFOUSEY, and was surprised—again—by the positive response. I was sitting outside in nature by a tree and cautiously trying to explain that I was ready to start to fight for my life again. I felt like I'd been given a second chance and knew that I had to seize it, so I kept posting vlogs.

At the time, I still had no place in LA and was still staying with my girlfriend. In an attempt to feel like I was making progress, I decided to use the little money I had left and lease myself a new car. A Toyota C-HR. I was now mobile. In case you were wondering, when I was in New Jersey, I was forced to sell the Ferrari 488 losing over $300,000 in the process. And just to turn the Range Rover Sport SVR back in, my dad was forced to write a check for $25,000 to break the lease early. I promised I would find a way to pay him back. I had lost all my money that year and was on my last remaining dollars. My dad wanted me to save them. There was a giant fear that I would have to sell the house in New Jersey especially since I had no more sources of income and YouTube no longer seemed like a possible career choice for me.

Each day I would wake up, go to Coffee Bean, grab a coffee, and to make myself feel like I was doing something, go to one of my YouTube buddies' houses and chill with him and his posse in private. I was never the same person around them as I no longer was the same person. The old me that would bring light to the room and make everyone laugh could barely get a few words out and laugh quietly at their jokes.

It was time I started to make a change so I reluctantly hit up every single old manager or agent I had known in LA. No one was willing to work with me or even pick up my calls except for one. The same manager who got me the opportunity to write this book. For that, thank you Kendall. You will always be a reason for my rebirth. She soon got me a gig to perform stand-up comedy at the Irvine Improv. I advertised it on my channels and invited all the of my closest YouTube friends. If we're being honest, not many showed up. A lot of people had decided to distance themselves from me in order to protect their brand and likability on social media. Being friends with Fousey just wasn't the cool thing to do anymore. This was my chance at redemption.

When the time came to head over to the venue, I was so nervous I felt sick. Would someone call in another bomb threat?

Would anyone even show up? The feeling got even worse when I arrived and discovered the show was sold out. But as I stepped out onto the stage, it was like I'd managed to get back to being my old self for the first time in two years, and I managed to deliver one of the best stand-up performances of my life. It was a total success.

With the little money I earned from that event, I rented an apartment in Studio City and had enough money to cover a few months' rent. I had recently decided to break up with my girlfriend because I had to be honest with her and myself. Her being with me at my lowest was only going to continuously hold her back from achieving her dreams and getting to where she needed to go in life. I had a lot of personal work I needed to attend to and I wasn't in the capacity to love another person when I was barely able to love myself. It was time to take control and restart my life.

"Everybody has a plan until they get punched in the face."

—MIKE TYSON

THE BOXING INCIDENT

I enter the ring in an attempt to win myself back.

When I got a call from Adam Saleh's manager in the summer of 2019, I was immediately on edge because I hadn't spoken to him since he'd posted all those shitty videos about me.

But rather than trying to provoke me, he said, "I have a proposal.... I want you and Adam to have a boxing match in London; it's a chance to put your differences aside once and for all. All the proceeds will go to charity, so it'll be great PR for both of you. You'd have a lot of goodwill, and it's a great way to fix your beef. So, what do you say?"

My immediate thought was that it was both a good and bad idea. Good because it could help mend my damaged reputation and relationship with Adam whom I'd always cared for and loved but bad because I'd be up against the wrong opponent. In addition to having a successful YouTube career, Adam was also an experienced amateur boxer. I'd never even tried boxing, and I had absolutely no talent for fighting.

"Give me some time to think about it," I told his manager. I still wasn't completely sure when I called him back a few days later.

"Before I make a decision," I said, "I need to speak to Adam on the phone."

He said he would check with Adam and get back to me. Not long later, he called me again, "Adam says it's cool. He'll reach out in a little bit."

When Adam called, it was exactly one year since we had last spoken, and the first thing he did was apologize for the videos he'd made about me. For my part, I took the chance to straighten out the misunderstandings my dispute with his manager had led to and apologized for not just doing the right thing and continuing the tour with him. I realized that Adam found the whole thing as liberating as I did, and we decided to kill our beef.

Still, I didn't want to fight him, and that's what I told his manager when I called him back a while later.

The minute I hung up, I had an idea. Adam Saleh had a friend called Slim Albaher, aka Slimmofication. He was a skinny guy from New York, and he didn't know a thing about boxing, or so I thought. I called Adam's manager straight back and said, "Yo, if you want, I'll box Slim on the undercard."

"Oh my God!" he said. "That's such a good idea. Let me see if Slim is down for that."

As it happened, Slim liked the idea too, and when I called him to make sure he didn't think I wanted a real beef, he said, "Don't worry, man. I never had a problem with you. But when it comes to boxing and we're in that ring, I want you to try to break my nose. I want a real fight."

The minute we signed the contract in early July, setting a date for the fight in September, I announced the news. I didn't even have to look for a boxing coach. Almost immediately, I got an Instagram message from a guy called Ricky Funez. He wrote, "Hey, I heard you're looking for a place to train. You could train at our place."

The place was Ten Goose Boxing Gym in Van Nuys, and I went over there the very next day.

I met Ricky and his nephew, Juan Funez, the trainer there, and explained that I really wanted to go all-in ahead of the match, but they didn't seem convinced. Maybe it was because it wasn't the first time someone had come in with a similar story, only to lose all interest once they realized how hard it actually was.

Either way, they gave me my first training session, and when I showed up at eleven on the dot the next day, they smiled. With each session I did after that, following their every instruction, they began to show me more and more respect.

My entire life suddenly revolved around building myself up again, and not just physically—I also had to rebuild my self-respect. I had to learn how to believe in myself and to find meaning in life, and that's what Ricky and Juan helped me to do at Ten Goose Boxing Gym.

Since I was there every day, we also got to talk quite a bit, and when they learned that I was doing the charity bout for free, they were shocked.

"You're kidding," said Ricky, giving me a suspicious look.

I was sitting down to catch my breath, but I shook my head. Ricky continued, "Listen to me, man—just because it's for charity doesn't mean no one's earning money from it. You're risking getting your face demolished, so you should get paid for that. I'm sorry, but you don't understand the business."

He was probably right there, and I think he felt sorry for me, because from that point on he refused to take any payment for my sessions. In exchange, I posted videos of our training work at his gym on my fouseyTUBE channel (which I had been trying to revive).

Every day, I mixed strength training with sparring. I was literally boxing the anger, pain, and frustration out of myself. In the evenings I would go running with Juan for a minimum of three miles. The whole thing became a kind of therapy for me because we talked a lot during our runs, not least about my feelings and worries about the upcoming fight. Juan helped me understand how to be my own friend.

"Having one opponent in the ring is more than enough," he said.

At the gym, Ricky got me to fight against professional boxers, so I would have a better idea of what awaited me. Those guys played around with me easily, of course, but they also allowed me to throw punches, boosting my self-confidence. Before long, I felt confident enough to invite my friend, also a YouTuber, to come to the gym and spar against me. I also invited a hundred or so fans to watch, and as I climbed into the ring that day, I wasn't just motivated, but in the best shape I had been in years. All my training, combined with a strict diet, meant I had lost a bunch of weight, and I remember feeling really pleased with how I looked for the first time in a long time.

Sadly I was brought crashing down to earth almost as soon as the first round started. My friend was beating me up like a punching bag, making it look like I hadn't learned a single thing during all my training.

When I returned to my corner, Ricky was agitated. He shouted, "What are you doing? This is nothing like we practiced. You're not keeping your hands up; you're not doing any of what we told you to do."

I felt genuinely ashamed as I sat there, and when the second round began, I was so disappointed and angry with myself that I charged out like a raging bull. That took my friend by surprise. He was immediately on the defensive, and I quickly knocked him down with a single punch and was left standing there as the winner. That gave me a sudden surge of self-confidence, and I was on cloud nine for the rest of the day.

When Juan showed up at my house for our run that evening, he had a big grin on his face.

"I still can't believe how well you fought today."

Juan, Ricky, and I flew to London ten days before the fight. The airline lost my luggage, meaning I couldn't train for the first three days, but I didn't care. I'd managed to adjust to the new time zone before I began doing daily training sessions in a boxing gym near the hotel. My baba, eldest brother Mohammed, and nephew Saleh were staying in the same hotel, along with a couple of my friends, including Alex Wassabi. Unfortunately, Slim was also staying there, as was Adam Saleh and everyone else connected to the fight. It meant the atmosphere was pretty charged because Slim and I now had a real beef, which was exactly what I hadn't wanted.

Sure, back while I was training in LA I had talked shit about him in my videos, saying things like "Everyone get ready for September 29th because you're gonna see me knock out Slim in the first round." Almost every morning. My ego was talking for me and I genuinely thought I would knock Slim out easily and at the same time was promoting the fight. What I hadn't realized was that being so focused on how I would knock my opponent out meant I found it completely impossible to keep my cool when I eventually saw him. Slim seemed to feel the same way, so we both took every chance we got to psych each other out.

At the press conference, for example, Slim told me, "Do you know what people from Muslim Twitter think about you? They hate you. You're a laughing stock. You're a joke. Nobody likes you. You are an embarrassment to Islam."

I knew he was trying to knock me off balance, but his words still took root in my head because they touched upon my greatest fear: being disliked.

Despite that—and despite everything Slim said the next day at the weigh-in—I tried to stay focused on the fight, and when I woke up on the morning of the match, I felt both confident and hopeful. That was probably partly because of the people around me, who kept telling me I'd easily win with a knockout. But it was also because I had learned during the weigh-in that I was both heavier and bigger than Slim and because I'd been doing so well during the last few sparring sessions.

When we went to the arena that day (me, Baba, my brother Mohammed, and my nephew), we were all in a good mood. Unfortunately, my anxiety kicked in when I got to the changing room, which reminded me of the film *Creed*. It was small and shabby with bare concrete walls dotted with flaking paint. My family and friends crowded in there with me and helped pick up the mood. Ricky bound my hands and tied my gloves, and I started warming up. Before long, I noticed that I was making the same mistakes I had at the very start of my training.

Ricky turned to me, "What are you doing?"

"I don't know," I said. "My head's just not right. But I got this, I got this."

That wasn't true. Rather than keeping calm and composed, I started hyperventilating, seething with some kind of crazy rage, and before I knew it, it was time for my ring walk.

Baba had asked if he could join me, so I walked out with my hands on his shoulders, which were draped with a Palestinian flag. The minute we stepped into the arena, which was sold out, I heard someone yell: "Fousey, we hate you! Die!"

Someone else joined in: "You're gonna lose, you piece of shit!"

Right then, I remembered all the crap Slim had thrown at me during interviews, and I felt a new and even stronger wave of anger mixed with nerves. My body began to shake, and my eyes started to well up with tears. I was anything but composed, in other words, and didn't hear a word Ricky said as I climbed into the ring.

Things didn't get any better when Slim came out and started dancing around me, horsing about and throwing mocking comments my way. Before I knew it, he was in my corner, and I leapt up from the stool and yelled in his face.

"Get back to your side!"

Ricky grabbed my arm and said, "What are you doing? Don't let him get to you. Calm down!"

Juan's head was in his hands as the judge called me into the middle of the ring. Just as I was about to start walking, I realized something was wrong. I turned to Ricky.

"I can't feel my legs."

His face turned white. "Don't fucking say that."

"OK," I said, staggering over to the judge. I touched gloves with Slim and then limped back over to my corner, completely drained of all energy. My adrenaline had been completely dumped.

As the bell rang and the fight started, my mind went completely blank. I forgot everything I'd learned, and made stupid mistake after stupid mistake. My arms were by my sides, for example; I didn't even *try* to defend myself for the entire fight. I also started throwing punches at random, while also receiving a series of blows to the face.

I was so angry and high on adrenaline that I didn't even notice when my nose broke—once, then another two times. I just kept going in like a madman, making zero attempt to maintain any kind of defense. In the end, after I'd gotten my ass beat four rounds in a row—all the while refusing to fall—Juan threw in the towel to bring an end to my suffering.

I saw Slim and his team start leaping around the ring in celebration and then I watched as the judge raised Slim's hand in the air.

Amir Khan, the former welterweight champion, held out a microphone to me, but I could barely manage a single word. Less because of my mashed nose than all the frustration and disappointment that made my throat contract.

Juan and Ricky led me back to the changing room, where I called my mama, who had been watching the match on my YouTube channel along with a whole load of my subscribers. My mind turned to all those people who had been watching, and it felt like the ground opened up beneath my feet.

I heard Mama's desperate voice: "Yousef, what did you do? Why didn't you defend yourself?"

I broke down in tears. "I don't know, Mama. I don't know."

"You, me, or nobody is gonna hit as hard as life."

—ROCKY BALBOA

NOSE SURGERY

*World famous plastic surgeon Dr. Jay Calvert
does what he can to fix my broken face,
and I reinvent MTV Cribs.*

It's difficult to describe just how resigned I felt in the days after the fight. I had been given an opportunity to defend myself and my honor and show everyone what I was capable of, but it had ended in yet another loss for me.

150,000 people had followed the fight live on my YouTube channel, and my family and friends had crowded into the arena. No one could believe what they had seen. Slim, the underdog, who weighed no more than 160 pounds, had not only beaten me, he'd put a stop to the fight—and to all dreams I had of fighting again in the future. In my head, I had imagined similar bouts against people like Jake Paul, who was one of the biggest YouTubers at the time, and plenty of others. Instead, I realized I would have to spend a bunch of time and money on nose reconstruction surgeries instead.

Immediately after the fight in England, I still hadn't processed just how bad it was.

My nose just felt so congested. Still, it was only once I got to the locker room and saw my reflection in my phone that I realized my nose was four times bigger than it was supposed to be.

Baba and Mohammed had followed me in.

Mohammed had gone through med school to become an Oral and Maxillofacial Surgeon, and he gave me a concerned look and said, "I think we should take you to the hospital now, to see if they can snap it back into place."

Half an hour later, I was sitting in the waiting room at a hospital nearby. My whole face hurt so much, but I still took a picture of my nose and uploaded it to Instagram, writing, "You win some, you lose some. That's just how it happens. At the end of the day I gave it my all. Trained as hard as I possibly could in two months and came prepared…I love you all…and massive congrats to Slim. You came, you saw, you concurred. Enjoy the win bro, you deserve it. PS. My nose was bad before I had it broken. So screw you for that."

I knew I'd be a laughing stock online no matter what I did, so I decided that uploading a picture was a way to get one step ahead of all the haters.

Before long, a doctor came to examine me. He took one look at my nose and said, "You need surgery…. There's nothing we can do at this point."

I flew back to LA with my broken nose the next day, and Mama and Baba came to stay with me while I waited with the doctor.

The thing was, I'd booked an appointment with a famous plastic surgeon named Dr. Jay Calvert two years or so earlier, hoping for a nose reduction. But after everything that happened on July 15, that plan had gone up in smoke. I called him again and when I finally went to his office, he told me, "Yousef, this looks really, really bad." After examining my nose for a couple minutes, he went on. "Your nose is totally deconstructed. This won't be easy."

He booked me for surgery a few weeks later, and once that was over, I had to wait four months before I could have another operation to redefine and reshape my nose. I took the opportunity to document the whole thing, uploading it to YouTube. I was also a guest on Logan Paul's Impaulsive Co-Host Mike Majlak show, talking through what happened and joking about it while gasping for air because I still couldn't breathe through my nose.

The ironic thing about the whole fight and its aftermath is that it was for charity, so I didn't earn a penny from it. But it did cost me a whole bunch of money—that I didn't have—just to fix my nose. Not including the cost of flights for my team and boxing expenses.

Still, between the first and second operation, my creative juices finally started flowing again, and I decided to launch a project I would come to call YouTube Cribs. It was basically a reinvention of MTV Cribs and involved YouTubers showing me around their houses, talking about their cars and what they spent their money on. I realized, why not make content that isn't about me? People judge me for anything I post, so why not start posting content that revolves around other popular creators? It was a perfect plan.

I recorded the first episode with Logan Paul on November 4. The second episode was with Lance Stewart. Both got millions of views, but I only managed to convince another two YouTubers to take part and therefore had to shelve the whole idea before I'd even gotten started. The thing with YouTube and social media fame is, when you're hot and on top, everyone wants to work with you. But when you've gone through the public humiliation and downfall that I had gone through, they want nothing to do with you. People will only be willing to work with you if it's good for their brand or if they have something to gain from it. If not, good riddance.

"Sometimes you climb out of bed in the morning and you think, I'm not going to make it, but you laugh inside— remembering all the times you've felt that way."

—CHARLES BUKOWSKI

SPRING 2020

I rekindle an old idea.

Coronavirus took us all by surprise, and since I didn't have a girlfriend and had lost most of my friends during my long periods of depression, I decided to move back in with my parents in San Diego during lockdown.

My latest project with YouTube Cribs had ended as suddenly as it started—partly because I couldn't find any more YouTubers interested in taking part and partly because of the pandemic. In short, I was stuck on a one-way street with no idea what to do next. So, I left social media again and began looking for a new way to survive.

Over the next two months I had studied courses online on how to make drop shipping online businesses. I had seen ads of people saying they have made thousands a month from it and thought it was worth a try. I launched three businesses while at my parents' houses. Drop Blanket, selling weighted blankets. Yoga Plum, selling woman's yoga apparel. And Baby Strolly, an online retailer for baby strollers. All three seemingly failed at once. I don't regret trying though. Because for two months I was actively working toward something which at least helped me find a purpose in the mornings. But just like clockwork, as soon as they failed, depression struck.

Still, there was at least one positive that came out of the whole thing, and that's that Mama and I suddenly had time to talk again. Even though she's older now, Mama is still very positive and motivating, and when I started hanging about in the kitchen a few days after moving back in with her, she looked me deep in the eyes and said, "Yousef, you have your whole life ahead of you. There are so many people who love you." Then she told me to go for a walk.

"I don't have the energy," I said, burying my face in my hands.

"Yousef, get out of the house," she continued, literally shoving me toward the door. "You need to get some exercise."

I knew there was no point arguing with her and soon set off along the road from Mama and Baba's house.

The sun had just come up, and a couple gulls screeched from one of the rooftops. From the corner of one eye, I saw a lady coming up behind me. She was at least twice my weight and with much shorter legs. Despite all that, she zoomed straight past me. I remember it made my jaw drop, because it was like she had turned up just to prove that no matter what situation a person might be in, they're still out there doing whatever they can. They're still trying. That realization didn't fill me with joy, but it did give me a glimmer of hope, and when I got back home a while later and sat down at the kitchen table with a cup of tea, Mama said to me, "The past is done, Yousef. There's nothing you can do to change it. You have to look forward, and you have to focus on what you have now."

"I know, Mama," I said with a sigh. "But I have so many regrets. I regret paying $13,500 a month for a penthouse apartment when I should have just bought a house. I regret going to Australia, because if I'd never gone there, I wouldn't have flown to LA for July 15.... I haven't been the same since that day. My personality changed, and I don't have the same moods or sense of humor anymore. I'm not as enthusiastic about anything. I miss my old self. I miss the personality I used to have, the sense of humor, the belief in myself. I feel like I'm a shell of the person I used to be, like there's something wrong with me."

I know Mama was trying her hardest to understand me, but she just couldn't do it, and when I came down to the kitchen next morning and told her I was having an anxiety attack, she just thought for a moment before asking me, "Do you have COVID?"

"No, Mama, I don't have COVID. I'm having an anxiety attack."

She pursed her lips and shook her head.

"Then wash up and pray."

Not long after that, I was back in bed. For the first time in a long while, I had an idea. Strictly speaking, I'd had the idea when I went to Bali, but as I lay there in bed I decided to actually make it a reality. I called my then manager Kendall.

"I want to write a book," I said. "I want to write about everything I've been through, and, above all, about myself. Because I know there are other people like me out there, and if I can help a single person by telling my story, then I want to do it."

Two weeks later, I drove back to LA and went straight to Kendall's office in Beverley Hills to meet my coauthors to be, Martin Svensson and Leif Eriksson.

On the way I thought about what else I wanted to do with my life, and made up my mind to contact Abreezy to ask if he'd like to come and live with me in LA and do live Twitch streams together again. It was a shot in the dark, because we hadn't spent any time together in almost two years. But Abreezy said yes, and a week later he flew to LA.

Just like before, we'd broadcast live every night. The fans loved it, and we quickly got thousands of views. The only problem was that I started drinking loads of alcohol and smoking weed again.

For the next six months of 2020 during lockdown, I continued live streaming with Abreezy on Twitch. Each night in order to entertain a live audience and be a version of my older self, I would resort to drinking and smoking to the point of blacking out each night. Sure it was entertaining for the viewers, but it was damaging my career and reputation even worse than before. I would wake up each morning and not remember what I had said on stream the night before. Someone would then upload the clips of me onto YouTube with titles like, "fouseyTUBE Going Crazy On Drugs." Yes, it was the only source of income I had at the time but at what cost? I couldn't keep the gig up forever and eventually had to call it quits.

"I seem to have run in a great circle,
and met myself again on the starting line."

—JEANETTE WINTERSON

KENYA

Mama's prayers come true.

It was early in December 2020 when I got a call that would change not only my view of the world, but also my life.

"Hi Yousef, this is Sajjad from an organization called Muslims of the World. We're interested in inviting you to take part in a charity mission to Kenya."

It was early morning, and I had just woken up. "What's the COVID situation like there?" I managed to ask.

"You have a better chance of catching COVID in America than in Kenya; there are no tourists there."

"OK," I said. "And what are you planning to do there?"

"We're going to be performing cataract surgery, giving people their eyesight back. We also plan to provide hearing aids to deaf children. People with that type of disability struggle to get a good education there and find it hard to get married."

I thought the whole thing sounded great. "I'm in," I told him. "But I'm curious, I haven't mentioned Islam on any of my channels for years. I also drink and smoke online, and I talk about having sex before marriage. The Muslim community completely despises me."

"Yes," said Sajid.

"I mean, I literally don't do anything representative of Islam. Why the hell does Muslims of the World want me for this?"

"Well," he said. "Adam Saleh mentioned your name."

Adam and I hadn't spoken in several months for reasons I don't want to go into here, so that news really blew my mind.

"Here at Muslims of the World, we don't believe in cancel culture. We see the way the Muslim community cancels people in many different contexts, but we believe that everyone deserves a second chance."

After we hung up that day, I called Mama and Baba (and my siblings) to tell them about the conversation and my upcoming trip. They all told me how happy they were for me; they were convinced it would do me good.

For my part, I had no expectations at all. All I knew was that it felt good to be ending an otherwise crappy year in an interesting, exciting way.

Maybe that was why, over the next few days, I packed like I was going to Dubai for two weeks. Two suitcases full of stuff—shirts, pants, sweaters, God knows what else. My brother Ahmed (who's also a doctor) made sure I had the right vaccinations and plenty of malaria pills, as a bare minimum.

Before I knew it, it was time to fly to New York to meet with Adam and Slim at Adam's place. A representative from Muslims of the World also joined us. His name was Mufti Rafiq and since he was helping lead the entire trip, he gave us a talk that evening.

I remember that Adam, Slim, and I listened dumbstruck as he talked about the trip and Islam. My faith was something I'd always questioned, so I couldn't help but ask why they wanted me on board again. The answer Sajjad had given me when we spoke on the phone just didn't seem to explain it. Sure, everyone deserved a second chance, but hadn't I already been given enough?

Mufti Rafiq just smiled and said, "Yousef, I always used to watch fouseyTUBE and your "Middle Eastern Family" videos when I was growing up. Man, having someone like you to look up to meant so much to me as a Muslim kid."

That was obviously cool to hear, but I still didn't feel entirely convinced. Maybe because I knew what I was really like behind the scenes.

"I disagree," I said. "I mean, how can I be a good representative for Islam when I openly drink and smoke and talk about sex online?"

Mufti smiled again and said that if I knew about his past, I would realize that the only difference between myself and others was that my sins were public, whereas everyone else kept theirs private. With that, the conversation was over.

Early the next morning, we flew to Nairobi, Kenya. The city was beautiful, and we checked into an amazing hotel. I remember thinking, "Damn, this is the sickest luxury vacation. Africa is dope."

Unfortunately, I soon realized that Nairobi was just a layover. The next day, we continued on to Wajir with nothing but a carry on containing two T-shirts and two pairs of pants; there was no room for anything else on the plane.

In many respects, Wajir looked like the desert. Nothing but sand. There were goats and camels on both sides of the gravel track we drove along and people carrying things on their backs.

The representative explained that we would be making a few stops before we checked into the next hotel, and before long, he stopped the car and climbed out.

Adam, Slim, and I followed him. On each side of the road, there was a small wooden building, and it wasn't until the guy pointed to one of them and said, "That's where the boys go," that I realized we were looking at a school.

There were a couple of kids standing by a water fountain in the yard, getting ready to pray. I walked over and tried to talk to them, but they didn't seem to understand English, so I had to make do with gestures and fist bumps.

A teacher came out and took us into one of the classrooms. There was almost nothing inside, and when I showed a few of the kids the basketball we'd brought with us, they didn't seem to know what to do with it; they tried to hit it like a volleyball.

As we set off for the hotel, we drove through an area where people lived in huts made from straw, often ten to a hut, without either a bathroom or a toilet. Walking around, I quickly realized that there weren't any food stores or cars either.

The hotel we were staying in was called the Wajir Palace Hotel, and since the representative had told us it was the best place in town, I was looking forward to it. Or I was until we pulled up outside, and I was struck by the different definitions of luxury. To those living in the area, I'm sure it was a luxury hotel, but for us Americans—any Westerners, really—it looked more like a ramshackle barrack.

I remember staring around, wide-eyed when I was taken up to my room. The air was damp and the place smelled of mold, and when I looked up at the ceiling, I saw there was water dripping from the AC unit.

I lay down on the bed and thought about how I was going to upload everything I'd filmed that day. I quickly realized that my viewers would feel sorry for the people here and then simply move on with their lives, and I felt like I wouldn't have achieved anything.

Right then, I had an idea, and I called the representative from Muslims of the World.

"Do I have your permission to post a link for donations online?" I asked.

"Sure."

The minute we hung up, I hit record on my camera and told my followers all about why I was sharing the donation link and what the money would be used for.

The next day, there was a hearing aid event not far from the hotel. There were two huge tents, and hundreds of people had walked for hours from neighboring communities.

A doctor talked us through the process of fitting a child with a hearing aid, and then it was time for the first young boy to be registered. The doctor checked whether the problem was physical or neurological and carried out a decibel test to see how much hearing he had.

I followed the boy and his mother into the tent, where I helped him fit the hearing aid, and the doctor set it to the right level. The boy heard his mother say his name for the very first time and immediately started crying.

On our next day there, the doctors removed cataracts from some of the more elderly residents. They worked all day long, and the patients returned the next morning with patches over their eyes, waiting for someone to take them off.

The representative turned to me. "Yousef," he said, "why don't you take off this gentleman's bandage."

He nodded to an old man I had welcomed earlier that day.

"Sure," I said. I walked over to the old man and greeted him in Arabic.

He replied in his own language, and the interpreter said, "He thanks you for helping him."

I removed the bandage, and once I was done, the interpreter asked the old man whether he could see. He replied that he could see better than he had ever seen before, and then he started praying. When he finished, I asked the interpreter what he had been praying for.

"He prayed for you and wanted to thank you for what you just gave him," the interpreter replied with a smile.

I walked away, and as soon as I was out of sight, I dropped to my knees and cried.

I started thinking about how much time I had spent complaining about things that were completely meaningless. Setbacks and problems that paled in comparison to the issues people had there.

I looked up and saw an older woman beckoning me over.

I glanced over to the interpreter, who had followed me, and asked what she wanted.

"She wants to pray for you."

Again, I broke down into a deep cry. Why were they praying for me? What had I done? I was simply there to document the trip and to help raise donations. Yet, they were thanking me as if I was the one who had completed their surgeries. Their humbleness took me by storm and for the first time in nearly three years since July 15, I had felt awoken. I had felt reborn. I in that moment felt like everything I had gone through was to get me to this moment in time. Everything felt like it happened for a reason. And once again, I was ready to restart my life.

WHERE AM I NOW?

When I started working on this book I was in hell. I thought my career was over. I was desperate. I had no purpose. No identity. No idea what I was doing or what I was doing it for. Despite that, I had an idea of writing a self-help book; a motivational story. But the more I spoke to my coauthors, the more I realized the extent of the traumas I had been through, the size of my battles with depression and addiction, and that necessitated a very different type of story.

2020 was a bad year for a lot of people. But for me it turned out to be one of the best, or at least one of the most important years of my entire life. Because it gave me a chance to accept my past and to understand that I have no one else to blame but myself for everything that has happened to me. At the same time, I was also able to let go of my past demons and start looking forward, and on January 1st of 2021 I released my final video on my 10 million subscriber channel, fouseyTUBE. A music video called "RE-UP." "RE-UP" represents being able to come back from any setback life may throw at you. No matter how hard things get, no matter how low you may fall, no matter you not being able to see an escape from your current reality, there is always a chance to RE-UP and do things better than you ever have before. The reactions I got from my fans were more respectful and affectionate than ever before, and not long after that I started a brand-new channel from scratch for maybe like the tenth time called Fousey. I decided to ditch my old fame and name in the past and start brand new with zero subscribers.

Over the course of a decade I have attracted so many haters and people in my life who wanted to see me fail. I no longer wanted to cater to them and no longer wanted to allow them to have an opinion or voice over my life. I wanted to show the world who I am authentically after all my trials and tribulations and broadcast my real self to the world. I also wanted to start on a fresh slate and allow the people who want to see what I am up to in 2021. If it's meant to be to have people subscribe it will be.

When you hit thirty years old, you're supposed to start the next chapter of your life. Take all the lessons you have learned from your twenties, take all the money you saved and take your life to the next level. But when I turned thirty, I was forced to restart my life and begin my journey all over again like I had in 2011 at twenty-one years old and start fresh. I had no money saved, no investments, no resources to lean on. Instead of being angry at that fact, I look at is as a blessing. Let's say July 15 had gone well. Let's say Drake did show up and it was a massive success. Maybe I wasn't ready for the blessings life was ready to throw at me. I feel as though I needed to go through the growing experiences over the last three years to get to the position I am now in today. Because if the blessings come into my life now, they will be appreciated and respected in a whole different fashion than they would have in my past.

Most people on the internet love to tell me that my career is over. That I am irrelevant and that I need to go find a real job. The truth is, I know my life hasn't even begun. The experiences and fame I have been through were just lessons to get me ready for my next chapter in life. Where I will be able to execute my real purpose. Where I will be able to implement real change into people's lives and help people by letting them know they are not alone.

Right now, in 2021, you wouldn't believe how good of a place I find myself in. But just the other day, one week before having to submit the final version of this book, I had a severe panic attack. When I chose to release this book, it was because it was the only thing I had left in my arsenal. My life was over. The last thing I wanted to do was a chance to tell my story from my side and give people an inside look into the truth behind my entire life. As I type this, in all honesty, I want to scrap this book. I mean, life is going good right now. My new channel Fousey has already surpassed 100,000 subscribers. People are recognizing the growth I have been through. They see the change. Why release a book that brings up my past? Why tell people about the trauma I have lived through? Why make myself seem like such a miserable, depressed person?

The only answer I could give myself is…if this book is able to resonate with one person out there, then it was worth it. If it has the capacity to help at least one person, it was worth it. I want to eventually be able to use my voice to help those going through what I go through and what I have gone through. Let my pain and trauma be someone's lessons and hope for a better tomorrow. Because it always gets better. Everything in life happens for a reason. And me signing this book contract isn't an exception. Whatever good or bad comes from the release of this book was meant to be and will help shape what's next for my life.

Being bipolar, having severe depression, and being an addict will always be a part of my life. It's not something I can just wake up with and be free of and a lot of people have a hard time understanding that. Luckily, for the first time in nearly a decade of being on medications, I have found a good mix that has worked quite well for me. I have also found a nice routine and groove that works for my lifestyle. Do I still have bouts of depression? You bet. Do I still fall victim to my addiction? Yes, I do. But do I still continue to fight for a better tomorrow? You better believe it.

If there's one thing I can give myself credit for, it's refusing to give up. I have fallen more times than I can count and this book doesn't even scrape the surface of the lows I have been through. But no matter how hard life gets, no matter how much I mess up, no matter how many times it would be acceptable for me to throw in the towel and just give up, I just don't know how to. I often tell people, the only time your life is over, is when you tell yourself it's over. As long as you have the capacity to wake up and see a new day, you have the capacity to change the course of your life forever. It goes down to how bad you want it. And for some reason—even though I may not know what it even is—I want it bad. Real bad.

This book is called *Warning: This Is Not a Motivational Story*. But I can assure you…my next book will be a motivational story. Because my story isn't finished. It's just getting started.

With love,
Yousef Erakat

Kindergarten

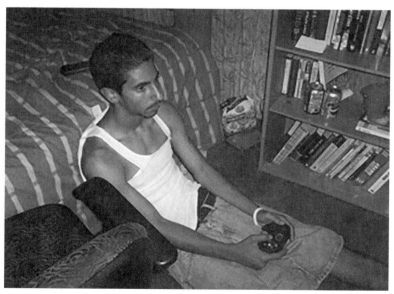

Teen Years

High School

Fraternity Days

Parents

College Plays

Dollar and Muffin

Dollar in Hospital

Dollar's Passing

Dollar's Memorial

Meeting Drake's Father

Meeting J. Cole

Meeting DJ Khaled

Rare Photo with Kanye

90 Day Journey

Bought My Parents a House

10 Million Subscribers

Roman vs Fousey Tour

Streamy Awards

Parents on Red Carpet

Depreciating Assets

High School Reunion

Project Butterfly

Australia, July 15th Inception

July 15th

July 15th

Boxing Match

Shoulder to Lean On

Kenya, Africa

Kenya, Africa

RE-UP

ACKNOWLEDGMENTS

Yousef Erakat thanks:

Firstly, I would like to thank every single one of you who picked up a copy of this book and gave me a chance to tell my own story. I know there is someone reading this right now who has been supporting me since I started my YouTube journey on March 25th of 2011. No matter how bad things got, you stayed with me and you were always with me to celebrate the high times. I would not be who I am if it weren't for your support.

I'd like to thank the entire Erakat family for always being my backbone. Even when I lost everything I had worked for in the decade of my twenties, you were still there for me and looked at me no differently. Mama, Baba, Ahmed, Noura, and Mohammed, I love you all endlessly and I hope to continue finding ways to make you proud throughout my lifetime. To be honest, I am terrified at the fact that you are reading the material in this book, but at the end of the day, I can't lie about my past and act as if it didn't happen. Hopefully we can all individually talk about this and allow me to elaborate on the issues I have suppressed my entire life.

It wouldn't be right to not thank my baby dogs Dollar and Muffin for at times being the only thing I had in life that allowed me to feel what love was. You gave me so much life and taught me so many lessons and I will forever cherish you. Dollar, I hope you are resting well and I want you to know that Muffin misses you and asks about you at all times.

I'd like to thank my role model, mentor, and friend Tyler Perry. You gave me a chance that changed my life forever. Outside of just giving me a role in a movie, you gave me a safe space to express my feelings and problems with no judgment. I will forever talk highly of you and always be grateful for the opportunities you opened up in my life.

Jermaine Cole, you may never get word of this acknowledgment, but you really are the spark that created everything I am today. Your music changed my life in more ways than one. I have followed your entire career and will always continue to do so. I was there when you opened up for Estelle at UC Irvine in the front row before the world knew of your talents. I listened to "The Come Up," "The Warm Up," and "Friday Night Lights" religiously throughout my turbulent life to get me through the hard times. I resonate with you on such a deep level and hope to one day be able to have a one-on-one conversation. I know I have met you before, but that was as a fan. Next time, I'd like for it to be as an individual.

Lastly, I'd like to thank every person I have come into contact with throughout my life. Whether we ended up on good or bad terms, you were a valuable part of my life and taught me lessons that helped me grow into the person I am today.

Martin Svensson and Leif Eriksson thank:

Yousef Erakat, our team, Alice Menzies, Neil Smith, Joel Berglund, Kristoffer Cras, our families and friends. All our publishers around the globe, particularly Permuted Press, and our great agent, Daniel Kim, at Arena Scripts Literary and Film Agency.

ABOUT THE AUTHOR

Yousef Erakat, also known as Fousey, is a YouTube personality, actor, and motivational speaker with over 15 million subscribers on his YouTube channels, over 21 million on social media, and over 1.7 billion views. In 2015, Fousey won "Show of the Year" for FouseyTube at the 5th Annual Streamy Awards. In 2016, he won "Entertainer of the Year" at the 6th Annual Streamy Awards for his daily vlog, "Dose of Fousey," and has toured worldwide with Roman Atwood. Yousef has starred in Tyler Perry's *Boo! A Madea Halloween*, and its sequel; YouTube Red's feature film, *We Love You*; Netflix's scripted comedy series, *Reality High*; and YouTube Red's *Fight of the Living Dead*. Yousef has partnered with AdBlitz, Verizon, Nike, Google, and Microsoft for major brand campaigns. He was listed third on the list of "40 Inspiring Muslims Under 40" by *MBMuslima Magazine*. Last year, he trained and appeared in his first boxing match for the "Fight Night" Charity Event in London to raise money for Yemen. Raised in the Bay Area, Yousef is of Palestinian descent. He attended San José University, where he earned his BA in theater arts and writing. Now, he's beginning to share his life story with the world and hopes to inspire others who might be facing similar battles.

ABOUT THE COAUTHORS

Martin Svensson and Leif Eriksson have written around forty books each, including both fiction and true stories. They started writing together in 2010 and have since produced a large number of official autobiographies for international actors, models, pop/rock stars, sports stars, and influencers.

Today, Martin and Leif have an established team of researchers and co-writers that they work with on a project-by-project basis.